The Mountain
Bike Book

First published in 2003
Reprinted 2006
Second edition 2009

A catalogue record for this book is available
from the British Library

ISBN 978 1 84425 673 0

Published by Haynes Publishing,
Sparkford, Yeovil, Somerset BA22 7JJ, UK

Tel: 01963 442030 Fax: 01963 440001
Int. tel: +44 1963 442030 Int. Fax: +44 1963 440001
E-mail: sales@haynes.co.uk
Website: www.haynes.co.uk

Haynes North America, Inc.,
861 Lawrence Drive, Newbury Park,
California 91320, USA

Printed and bound in England by
J. H. Haynes & Co. Ltd, Sparkford

Picture credits
Stockfile Chapters 1–6, 9 and cover,
Groundeffect Chapter 7, **Seb Rogers** Chapter 8
Madison Chapter 6

Author's Acknowledgements
With many thanks for solid and invaluable contributions from Jill Behr, Steve Behr,
Guy Kesteven, Mike Davis, Jez Loftus, Seb Rogers, Jo Young, Holly Young, Jane
Bentley and www.groundeffect.co.nz for the togs and action shots in Chapter 7.

The Mountain Bike Book

SECOND EDITION

Your guide to the history, bike types, fitness, riding technique, bike anatomy and maintenance essentials

Steve Worland

Haynes

Introduction

Many moons ago, in a monthly mountain bike mag, a celebrity mountain biker said 'Get out there, ride, and discover yourself'. It sounded to me like a bit of a cliché, but it stuck in my mind and continues to surface when I'm struggling to regain control on a muddy drop, grinning my way through swoopy single track or attempting to conquer another climb. It shouldn't need a sound bite from a celebrity to remind us mere mortals why we're doing what we're doing, but it often does.

Mountain biking is about a lot more than just cycling. It's about an apparent need to recapture the essence of personal control that's often lacking in modern lifestyles. The MTB might appear to be something of a misnomer: after all, most MTBs are pedalled through city streets rather than on the slopes of the mountains for which they were first intended. But here lies the secret and the beauty of the MTB. It's a true multi-use tool, a sort of two-wheeled adjustable spanner if you like, and it really does allow us to discover bits of ourselves and our geography that will remain redundant for much of the non-mountain biking populace.

We've been pedalling bikes on- and off-road for as long as bikes have been around. The MTB is still a relatively new addition to pedal-powered progress but, in a single generation, it's rekindled a spirit of adventure that makes us want to get to places under our own steam. It's done this at precisely the right time in the history of human mobility and escape, a time when motorised options seem to cause as many problems as they solve and walking simply doesn't offer enough excitement.

The MTB has completely reinvented the popularity of bicycles by making riding an easy, comfortable, pleasant and rewarding experience. For as long as we need to escape into the hills, forests and canyons of our minds, the MTB will always be one of the most glorious ways to do it.

Steve Worland

CHAPTER 1

The history of mountain biking

It seems amazing that the mountain bike is only a quarter of a century old. Its popularity has grown to a point where it's become the bike most people buy and ride, even if they never venture off-road. The technology that's evolved with the mountain bike has come to influence radical development in all other bike types, from workhorse shoppers to Tour de France race winning bikes. You can't help but wonder how different things might have been if the MTB spark hadn't ignited back in the 1970s …

On an early days mountain top, some denim clad conquering heroes shoot the breeze.

Big kids, big skids. Occasionally frowned upon, always fun.

How did it all start?

The history of the mountain bike is the stuff that legends are made of. It's a story of troublesome adolescence, mismanaged education, cul-de-sac love affairs and inspired maturity. It's a story of a gifted child, born in the '70s and reared by one of the most unlikely families you could ever hope to meet. It could easily have gone terribly wrong, but the spirit that coincidentally nudged the whole thing into action all those years ago is an enduring spirit. For as long as we need to escape into the hills, the forests and the canyons of our minds, the MTB will always be one of the most glorious ways to do it.

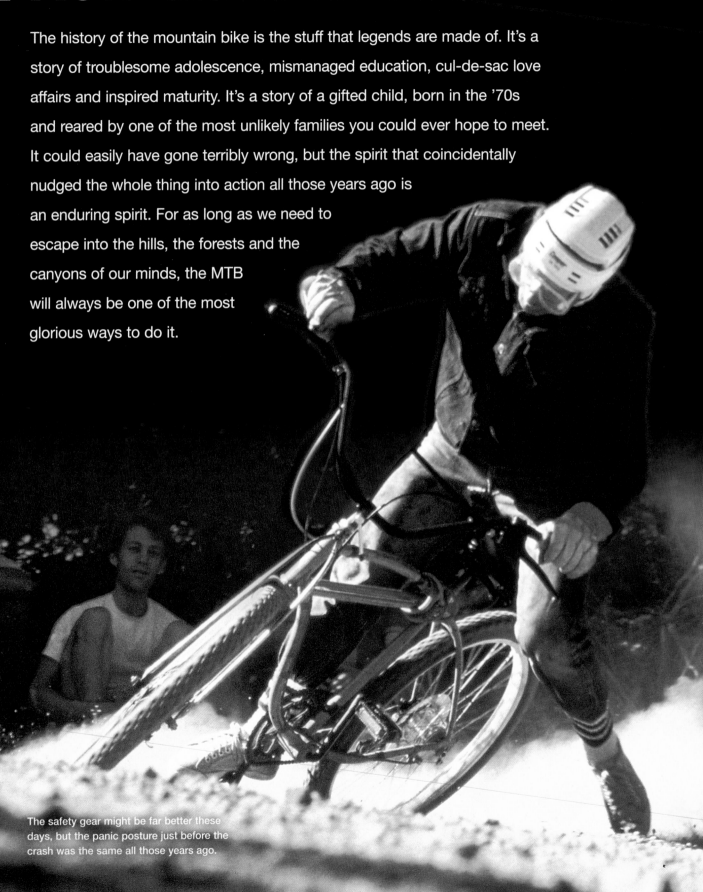

The safety gear might be far better these days, but the panic posture just before the crash was the same all those years ago.

The MTB heralded an age of bikes suitable for their intended purpose. Prior to MTBs the Rough-Stuff Fellowship were the UK masters of trail riding ... or pushing.

The mountain bike has 'officially' been around for about a quarter of a century. That's not long. Although people have been riding off-road for way longer than that, it was only in 1979 that Californians Gary Fisher and Charlie Kelly pooled all their cash (the grand total of $300) to form a company called MountainBikes. They attempted to protect the name, in its many forms, without any success, and it wasn't long before meddlers were trying to call them ATBs (All Terrain Bikes) instead of MTBs. But the MTB tag stuck, so on paper the mountain bike has existed since late 1979.

In the beginning . . .

While Gary Fisher is happy to be seen by the bicycle buying public as the inventor of the mountain bike, there have been all sorts of arguments in potential 'founding father' peer groups as to whether Gary has a rightful claim to paternity. And of course, at the end of the day it doesn't really matter. But it's interesting to look at the way the whole thing started.

In the US, the balloon tyred Schwinn Excelsior cruiser was seen as the bike that formed the basis of pre MTB off-road activity. It was built in the 1930s and was strong enough to take a hammering in the early '70s downhill races of California's Marin County Larkspur Canyon Gang. The late '30s versions of the Excelsior, with drum brakes, were popular but the strap-on front cantilever brakes of the '50s were the most sought after items. The rear coaster (back pedal) brakes of old cruisers would heat to grease-burning point on long downhills. The 'Repack' descent of Marin County mountain bike legend was so called because you had to repack your coaster brake with grease after every run.

In Europe, off-road riding in its racing form was cyclo cross. In its club form it was catered for in the UK by the Rough-Stuff Fellowship, a spin off from the Cyclists Touring Club. But kids everywhere were cobbling together bikes to ride off-road. Any one of them could have become the 'inventor of the mountain bike'. But they didn't. The sequence of events leading to the Mountain Bike tag being carved in stone was unexpected...

Milling around aimlessly discussing bike styles hasn't changed one bit in the last 20 years. Seems buses haven't either.

Becoming a force

The 1920s

Some will argue that the true inventor of the mountain bike was Arthur Clough, who cut the first knobbly tyres in his Barnsley, UK, scullery way back in 1927. Unfortunately, there is absolutely nothing to back up this legend apart from the oft-rumoured secret box of rubber shavings, kept under lock and key by Clough's grandson, an ardent anti-mountain bike campaigner. Until the late '70s, none of the people who claimed to have invented the MTB came up with a marketable name or image.

The early 1970s

Groups of riders in Marin County, California, were getting into the idea of bombing down hills around Mount Tamalpais on one-geared cruisers, or clunkers (sometimes spelt with a k) as they were often called. Gary Fisher was among many characters looking at ways of making the bikes more suitable for their intended purpose. At the same time a parallel group of riders from south of San Francisco Bay were riding what they referred to as 'bombers', cruisers with ten gears and decent braking instead of easy to burn out coaster brakes.

Charlie Kelly, early days business partner of Gary Fisher, shows his mettle, and natty limb-pads, on the Repack downhill run.

Scot Nicol, later to set up Ibis Cycles, attempts to eat lunch off his sparkling new cantilever brakes.

A gnarly looking modern-days Charlie Kelly shows off his historic leaflet advertising the infamous 'Repack Downhill Ballooner' races.

The mid-1970s

Around '75 the Marin crowd started putting gears on their clunkers. It's been suggested that this was a result of South Bay riders riding a Marin County cyclo cross race. The race drew a mix of traditional cyclo cross bikes and clunkers. In the mid '70s a market for converted multi-geared clunkers was emerging. Enthusiast builders began collecting truck loads of parts from back yard bike shops in neighbouring states. A restored clunker with decent brakes and derailleur gears sold for around $400.

The famous Repack downhill races were held in Marin County between '76 and '79. While Joe Breeze won the most races (10), Gary Fisher set the course record (just over 4 minutes). Repack was a killing fields for clunkers. It forced new innovation. The bikes got stronger, the brakes and gears got better.

The late 1970s

In '77 and '78 Jo Breeze built some frames for the growing 'enthusiast' clunker market. They were called Breezers and they were stronger and lighter than the old Schwinn Excelsiors. It was the beginning of a new custom-built off-road bike market. The early bikes weighed nearly 40lb (18kg), mainly because of steel rims and heavy tyres. Fitted with an eclectic selection of components, including Phil Wood hubs and bottom brackets, Dia Compe cantilever brakes, Magura motorbike brake levers, TA cranks (double or triple), SunTour thumbshifters

and Shimano or SunTour gear mechs, these bikes sold for $750. Joe Breeze was, for all intents and purposes, the first person to build a mountain bike from scratch.

Motorcycle builder and racer Mert Lawill, who was later to design some of the most innovative full suspension systems for MTBs, was around at this time too. His multi-geared Lawill Pro Cruiser, built in '78 and sold in the hundreds, was based on a frame made by the Koski brothers of the Cove Bike Shop in Marin's Mill Valley. The Koskis had a fast developing reputation as the specialist parts centre for off-road aficionados.

In '79 Gary Fisher ordered three custom frames from Tom Ritchey, a 20-year-old racer and frame builder. Tom had ridden the Repack race, so he knew what was needed. Gary then ordered nine more, at $450 each for a frame and forks. In Marin the market was booming. Fisher and Kelly set up 'MountainBikes', the first company devoted purely to MTBs. Ritchey continued to make the framesets. Whole bikes sold for about $1,300.

As the market grew, Fisher and Kelly started buying frames from other builders. Then rim makers Araya and Ukai introduced 26 inch alu rims. It was the turning point. The new rims resulted in a big weight saving and greatly improved the power of the now popular Mafac cantilever brakes. When good tyres started to appear on the scene, the early Ritchey-built MTBs were down to 28lb (12.75kg) in weight, not much different to MTBs today.

Full steam ahead

The early 1980s

At the '81 Long Beach bike show, 15 custom builders showed their MTBs. In the same year Mike Sinyard from Specialized Bicycle Imports bought four Ritchey-built bikes. They used the design as the basis for an order to Toyo, their Japanese production facility. A short time later the first Specialized Stumpjumpers were in shops. Unfortunately, due to a mix up about fork length on the bikes Sinyard had bought from Fisher and Kelly, the forks on the first batch of Stumpjumpers were too long, creating a very laid back geometry. Still, no one knew what was right or wrong in these early days, 500 were sold in stores through '82 for $750 each. This was about the same amount of bikes that Fisher, Kelly and Ritchey had assembled and sold between them in '81.

The amateur bubble was about to burst. Corporate bike companies were all looking for a way of jumping onto the MTB bandwagon. The Japanese were sending groups of besuited spies over to ask questions around the stores and the blossoming race scene. US based Univega was one of the first on the corporate bandwagon. Their Alpina Sport, made in Japan by Araya, sold 3,000 units in '82 for $500 apiece.

The amount of custom builders coming into this new market was still increasing, but '82 was their last year of domination. The likes of Joe Breeze, Mert Lawill, Scot Nicol (Ibis), Steve Potts (WTB), Erik Koski (Trailmaster, today Koski Engineering), Charlie Cunningham (Indian, today WTB), and Jeff Lindsay (Mountain Goat) were entering the market as relative smallfry in a giant melting pot of corporate ambition.

The Stumpjumper is still in the range of Californian pioneers Specialized. Inevitably, it bears no resemblance to this first offering, a heady mix of insectile road and fat tyred clunker technology.

By 1983, the mountain bike was being absorbed into mainstream bike culture in the US. MTB sales accounted for 5 per cent of the market. Two years later it was up to over 30 per cent and ten years later it was a massive 95 per cent. In '83 Shimano released their first, and still revered, Deore XT groupset. SunTour introduced Mountech. Triple cranksets were becoming the norm and the Japanese had started to make major progress in a componentry industry previously dominated by the European manufacturers.

As '83 progressed, it became obvious that all was not well with the old Fisher-Kelly-Ritchey arrangement. By the end of the year, Ritchey was back on his own and Fisher had bought Kelly out (apparently for an Apple computer and $2,300). Fisher was looking towards bigger scale far east production as a way of climbing out of his company's increasing debt.

As MTBs became big business, economies of scale created two separate markets: the mass produced bikes and the custom bikes. The builders who were to survive in the custom market were the ones who had sound business sense and an eye for the sort of fine detail that would be seen as both innovative and worthwhile. Innovation alone was not enough.

As the US market gathered steam, Euro manufacturers started dabbling in MTB manufacture. They'd had their fingers burned by the storm in a teacup that was the early BMX years, so they weren't full of optimism about the MTB trend.

The bike market in Europe was in a fairly moribund state, all but dead where profits were concerned. Despite the popularity of big road race events like the Tour de France, car culture dominated the economy and bikes were seen as old fashioned. Only real enthusiasts actually rode bikes. Most people were emerging from childhood without a glimmer of interest in riding a bike.

Meanwhile, over in the US, the MTB market was booming and there were experiments going on with new materials. Merlin Metalworks were building a great reputation for their titanium frames. The prolific early racers like Joe Murray were linking up with manufacturers to promote their products and help in the design process. Murray, whose first race was the 1983 Rockhopper Classic, went on to win 60 races in five years. As a pro rider and expert consultant, he worked his way through Fisher, Merlin, Marin, Brodie, Kona and Shimano.

Slowly but surely, the early star riders who emerged through the cross country race scene were being replaced in the public eye by the likes of John Tomac, the first real superstar of the MTB scene. Emerging from a BMX background, he became one of the only riders to come close to being World Champion at both cross country and downhill racing. Juli Furtado almost managed the same, but it was the flamboyance of Tomac that captured the public imagination. It was almost Tomac alone who made it possible for racers to earn a living from sponsorship money.

Joe Murray, possibly the most succesful racer ever, worked with the likes of Fisher, Merlin, Marin, Brodie, Kona and Shimano. He set the scene for top racers influencing bike design. These days, 20 years after his MTB career began, he's just started building his own frames.

A social phenomenon

Euro milestones

The United Kingdom led Europe into the MTB revolution. What happened in the UK was essentially what happened a year or two later in other western European countries, and what's only today starting to happen in the eastern European countries that missed out on the initial MTB boom.

The company that launched MTBs on the British scene, pre-empting the Euro scene, was Muddy Fox. An unlikely pairing of a Scottish marketing man, Drew Lawson, and a Cypriot accountant, Aristos Hadjipetrou, set up Muddy Fox in '82. At the time there were thought to be about 200,000 MTB owners in the US, but people in Europe hardly knew of them.

Muddy Fox's first delivery of bikes were built in Japan by Araya, better known as rim makers. The first bikes were badged with the destined-to-fail name of 'S & G Distributors'. This fast became Muddy Fox, a bizarre mis-translation from Japanese to English of 'Joy Bike'. Don't laugh, the French version of the MTB was called 'Funny Bike' for a couple of years before a new definition, VTT (Velo Tout Terrain), took over. Elsewhere in Europe, the name 'Mountain Bike' stuck. Muddy Fox took a paw print for their logo, taken from an Old English Sheepdog in the pub near Muddy Fox's office one night.

The company was aiming high. The average price of a Muddy Fox bike was £450 and there was a limited edition £1,000 bike to use purely for hype. Interest in the MTB from the public at large was symbolised by the fact that they received orders for the £1,000 bike. But they still didn't do too well until early in '85, when a switch to Taiwan assembly introduced the £300 Courier. It proved to be a watershed: the £300 price tag was acceptable to most people, cyclists or not, and suddenly bikes were no longer the outmoded transport of the social underdog. In '87 Muddy Fox sold 20,000 bikes. The MTB had hit the mainstream grade in the UK market three or four years after the US.

The success of UK market pioneers Muddy Fox was founded on their bikes being used by London couriers as well as off-road. Fashion was almost out-running technology as an MTB driving force.

UK bike engineers Pace started up in 1986. Their superb RC100 bike set brave new design parameters for MTB technology.

The early UK MTB scene was driven by an unusual cross-section of types who, five years earlier, would have had very little in common. Very few of them would have even been cyclists if the MTB hadn't come along. The likes of Muddy Fox were marketing the imagery of the MTB in ways that captured the imagination of a style conscious generation. Bike couriers and commuters were choosing the MTB for its durability and easy riding comfort. A rapidly blossoming race scene was drawing in fresh riding talent as well as those from other cycle sport disciplines.

At the same time, cycle shops and entrepreneurs were looking to America for new bike and componentry designs and the presumed 'exclusivity' of US branded products that home brands like Saracen and Ridgeback would never quite capture. The US market leader Specialized started exporting to the UK, closely followed by Fisher, Cannondale, Marin, Trek and GT. By the late '80s, almost every major US brand was represented in the UK.

In the late 1980s, the 'traditional' UK custom frame building game jumped on the MTB bandwagon but, like the small US builders, they would never go big scale successfully. Through word of mouth marketing, the likes of Dave Yates, Bromwich, Overburys, Chas Roberts and several others who'd emerged from the road scene, were putting out top quality products in small numbers. But the real hype surrounded all the US brands. At the top of the market, the likes of Fat Chance, Merlin, Salsa, Rocky Mountain, Manitou and Bontrager were approaching frame building from an enthusiast rider's point of view. Many of them were working in tandem with top MTB racers to develop their designs, and the builders were becoming back-street heroes to countless riders.

In 1988 Yorkshire based Pace Research Cycles arrived. They became the focus for a magazine blitz on a UK MTB success story. Formed by Adrian Carter and Duncan MacDonald, both top off-road competition motorbike riders, Pace were a UK version of US innovators Manitou. The parallels were manifold: motorcycle background, a frame that used box section alu tubes and, within a couple of years, a top suspension fork that could rival (at least at local level) the market-dominating RockShox brand.

The early '90s were the development years for suspension forks. At the 1990 World Championships in Durango, Manitou and RockShox launched the suspension fork revolution. Pace may have been the first to make a fork that came close to 3lb (1.4kg) in weight, but demand for Pace's products would always outstrip supply. Like so many other MTB cottage industry firms, they were destined to stay small compared to the likes of RockShox or Manitou, but their product range was, and still is, unique. Their RC100 frame, designed in '87, has almost the same geometry as the now much mimicked Gary Fisher Genesis geometry 'revolution' of the late '90s.

Few other frame makers were to make the grade in the UK. In fact, even Pace have never really made money on frames. The suspension fork has been their real success story. Other UK componentry entrepreneurs like USE, Hope, Middleburn, and Crud Catcher climbed on-board the bandwagon, but the main impetus of the MTB market by the mid '90s was mass sales of far east produced complete bikes and copycat accessories.

In mainland Europe, the UK pattern was being repeated. Countless framebuilding concerns were springing up and the big road-biased components manufacturers were increasingly turning their attentions towards MTB kit. While the road scene remains big at racing level in Europe, MTBs or their hybrid offspring are the dominant sales factor.

Pace co-founder Duncan MacDonald welding one of the early RC100 box section aluminium frames.

Go anywhere, ride anything

Bouncing into the future

After the meteoric initial blossoming of the MTB market, the technical innovations came thick and fast. Geometry changes were incorporated subtly into frame designs, steel parts became aluminium parts and the quest to lose unnecessary weight became almost as intense as it was on the road race scene. Before long, cross country racers were on bikes that resembled laid-back road racing bikes with flat handlebars and big tyres. New frame tubing designs meant that MTB race frames weighed only a few ounces more than road race frames.

The idea of creating a suspension fork was initially frowned upon by all but the most open minded racers, and as it tended to be the racers who called the shots in the early days, it took a while before RockShox, the small US company founded by Paul Turner, made any real progress.

It was the growing popularity of downhill racing that set the futures of RockShox and Manitou forks. They soon became must-have items on any self-respecting rider's shopping list and, although some die-hard cross country racers persevered with rigid forks in order to save weight, the idea of rear suspension was starting to attract a lot of attention in the downhill race circles.

Early rear suspension offerings were comfortable but overwhelmingly inefficient in terms of pedalling. Trek managed to effectively produce a triangulated pogo stick while Off Road, soon to be called Pro Flex, came up with the Flex Stem and an elastomer supported back end that, while way better than most of the opposition, fish tailed alarmingly and did a fine job of persuading many riders to stick with the good old fashioned hardtail. However, within a year or two, Pro Flex and many others were improving their designs.

The fast progression of suspension forks signalled that it was time for all the brains to shift gear into solving the follow-through problems of rear suspension. It wasn't long before air sprung hydraulically damped rear shocks were developed and the likes of GT and Mountain Cycle had created chassis designs for them to plug into. Within another

Massed start cross country racing is still popular but the emphasis these days is just as likely to be on single-loop marathon events as on multi-lap courses.

couple of years, everyone had put their pivot points in roughly the right place and suspension choices were basically being split into three camps: low maintenance single pivot unified rear triangle (drivetrain on the swing arm); low maintenance single pivot interrupted rear triangle (drivetrain on the main frame and gears on the swingarm); or four bar linkage (this usually involved a bit more maintenance and offered a baffling variety of linkage configurations and efficiency explanations). The popularity of unified rear triangle designs soon dwindled to insignificance and the design brains were finding ever more solutions to match the demands of increasingly discerning riders. (See 'Bike anatomy' for more details.)

As downhill and cross country bike designs moved apart, a growing band of ordinary riders were signalling that they did not necessarily want to ride race-designed bikes. The dominance of race-designed bikes started to ebb in the late '90s and more comfortable go-anywhere bikes started to emerge, typified by riser handlebars and a growing interest in front and rear suspension systems that could help to expand a rider's ability horizons. In other words, bikes that made you feel like you could ride a lot better. These bikes were effectively incorporating the best of both downhill and cross country riding technology.

With the advent of 'Freeride' or 'Enduro' bikes at the turn of the century, we effectively returned to the concept of fun bikes for gravity assisted riding, but with a bonus; now they were efficient enough and had enough gears to ride back uphill too … a bit like those old Marin County clunkers really, only far more sophisticated and much more fun.

The backyard builders have not competed well in pricing and marketing terms. By the end of the '90s most of the decade's early design and frame construction heroes were just ticking over. A few went corporate while maintaining their roots aspirations. Others have been bought into bigger companies, most famously the likes of Gary Fisher, Keith Bontrager and Gary Klein into Trek. Who knows what the future will bring?

There's a whole new generation of US hand-built frame designers up at the top end of the marketplace, and carbon-composite frame structures are increasingly making their presence felt as a new push for minimum weight flatters the increasingly efficient full-suspension bike designs.

Pace co-founder and racer Adrian Carter tackles a river crossing at speed on an early prototype downhill machine.

John Tomac, one of the only riders to ever mix cross country and downhill racing at top international level, races downhill at the World Championships in Vail, Colorado. He's now retired from racing and running his own bike company.

The leading edge

The racing scene, initially cross country then later downhill, drove MTB development from day one until the last few years. Now the comfort and fun demands of the average rider are seen as more important than the pure speed needs of racers. This move away from the race emphasis goes some way towards explaining why it's recently been increasingly difficult for racers to get good sponsorship deals. They are simply not needed as much as they used to be. Or perhaps the race thing has just got far too serious for its own good.

UK downhill-race star Steve Peat has been at the top of his game for ages, influencing and helping a whole generation of UK downhillers who now lead the world in most race categories.

Where have all the heroes gone? OK, there are still a few around, but it would appear that the current race scene, particularly the cross country race scene, has become too far removed from ordinary riding, which is now far better represented by the enduro/marathon event scene. Those likeable superstars who normal riders can relate to are a rare thing, but let's take a look at some of the stars who set the scene, many of whom have now disappeared or, like the UK's biggest star Steve Peat, are on the brink of 'retirement'.

In the early racing days, Joe Murray was a name that stood out among the stars, not only because of his prolific race results, but also because of the way he translated his ride abilities into bike design. His sloping top tube design is a characteristic MTB feature, and it's a feature that's cropping up increasingly on road bikes. Murray is still a consultant for various industry leaders.

John Tomac was, without a doubt, the racer who transformed his racing abilities into marketable propositions. His sponsorship deals and great ability to race both cross country and downhill at the highest level set him apart from almost everyone else. His off the bike character bears little resemblance to his flamboyant ride style. Tomac now helps to run his own bike brand.

Greg Herbold was the only one of the old-school downhill specialists who became fully involved in the whole product development deal. His world-beating riding skills and colourful character put him on a pedestal. Like Tomac, he spent his most successful years building his career in product development. These days, you'll often see him representing RockShox and the SRAM Corporation at races and shows.

Ned Overend is regarded by many as the king of cross country MTB racing. Now over 50, he's still winning from time to time against riders half his age. He's spent pretty much his whole career with Specialized and he's seen as the rock-steady XC racer every 40-something would like to emulate.

David Baker and Tim Gould, rarely separated in their early racing days, were the UK riders who broke through into the US scene. Gould was a climbing specialist who became a real hero to many US riders because of his ability to win at altitude. Baker was arguably the one who had the best chance of winning a World Championship. He came close a couple of times, but seemed more plagued than most riders with punctures.

Juliana Furtado was, for several seasons, way ahead of the opposition. She was also one of the very few riders to win both downhill and cross country races. She was struck down with Lupus disease, which forced her retirement.

The larger than life hype that surrounded the colourful persona of Missy Giove probably did more than anything to bring women's downhill racing to the same level of publicity as the men's race. Her flamboyance has always been the headline grabber,

but Giove was a highly skilled athlete who's always gone against the grain by stressing the fitness angle of downhill racing. Downhill racing needs characters like Giove to counter the almost predictable Championship winners like Nicholas Voilloz and Anne Caroline Chausson. A new generation of downhill and cross country racers has started to dominate, but with winning margins being counted in fractions of a second it's harder for a single athlete to dominate the scene.

Countless riders, far too many to mention, have become local heroes as the race scene has progressed over the years. Some have moved onwards and upwards to perform on the world stage, most notably top UK downhillers like Tracy Moseley and the remarkable Atherton family – Dan, Gee, and Rachel – and the guy who always seems to look ready to beat the world's best at cross country, Liam Killeen.

As a brave new breed of stars emerges, the old names fade, and some, most notably Cadel Evens, move sideways into a road-racing scene that can often earn them a better living. But being an MTB hero has little to do with winning races and money. Jason McRoy, the UK downhill racer who was a hero to almost everyone in the sport, rose up through world rankings when winning and earning were incidental to making your mark. He set the scene for the likes of Steve Peat to race abroad but, as he was reaching the peak of his career, he died in a motorbike accident. Where will the new heroes come from?

Tracy Moseley is one of the best downhill riders in the world, but constantly proves that being a superbly fit all-rounder is as important as any amount of technical skill and nerve.

He's won almost everything else, but Steve Peat is still waiting for his first World Championship win.

Where to next?

What will the future bring for the mountain bike? It's difficult to know. Superficially, we seem to have come full circle during the last quarter century, and that's probably a good thing. The early spirit still lives on. Those first 'real' MTBs emerged from the thrills and spills of downhill dirt riding. They sprouted more gears, got progressively lighter and got easier to ride because most riders preferred the option of riding, rather than pushing, back up the hills. Most of us expect our big thrills to come from gravity assisted trails, but most regular riders are fairly content to earn the reward, at least at an everyday local level, by getting up the hills under their own pedal power. Meanwhile, big ski resorts are seeing lift-fed downhill mountain biking as a summer tourist draw. There will always be room for both approaches.

Alpine ski resort MTB tourism is big business these days, and the bikes are built to take the rocky punishment.

'High Consequence Singletrack' provides a lot of the thrills in mountain resorts, so rider skills are firmly to the fore.

While we've seen increasingly function-specific bikes aimed at experts in the competitive arena, most riders still like to use one bike for most of their riding, although the desire of real MTB enthusiasts to own more than one bike is growing. It's not really need that triggers multiple bike ownership. It's high disposable income combined with an understandable obsession with technical progress and prowess – that seductive blend of positives that drives most consumer goods.

It seems inevitable that the near future will see increasing numbers of riders on lightweight full suspension bikes. Prices for good suspension technology have been dropping, pedalling efficiency has been increasing and we seem to be settling in for a period where having fun on a bike is becoming far more important than the tiny time gains made possible by minimalist weights. However, the best full suspension bikes at the top end of the market will continue to lose weight as more componentry is designed for bikes that are well cushioned from ground impacts.

At the same time as 'normal' cross country-biased full suspension bikes become lighter and more efficient, those riders who like to ride above and beyond the boundaries of 'normal' cross country will be catered for by the new breed of hard-knocks bikes. Such bikes will benefit greatly from new materials and new ways of working with materials and, while those buying bikes in the high price brackets will initially reap the rewards, it won't be long before some of the mass production benefits trickle down into bikes aimed at relative beginners. It's happened with frames, forks, gears, brakes, and most other componentry already. You can buy a bike costing roughly an average week's wages that now offers the performance advantages of a bike that only three or four years ago would have cost an average month's wages. This will continue to happen as the top-end bikes get even better.

CHAPTER 2

Mountain bike types

Mountain biking started with a bunch of bikes that weren't too well suited to their intended use. Since then, the development of the species has resulted in MTBs becoming thoroughbred go-anywhere do-anything bikes. While purist downhill bikes have evolved to a degree where the untrained eye might simply see them as motorbikes without engines, most other MTB genres have become completely accessible to ordinary riders. From town bikes to jump bikes, the MTB serves to please.

Only the sky sets the limit for some riders.

Some riders just live for the speed-rush of downhills.

Decent suspension systems have as much to do with landing from a height as they have to do with controlling bumps.

Downhill

It goes almost without saying that riding a bike at speed down hills is what mountain biking is all about for many riders. It's how it all began, it appeals to young and old alike and, while you obviously have to make your way to the top of the hill in the first place in order to savour the plummet, descending hills doesn't necessarily require athletic prowess, although you'd be surprised at how much training a downhill racer does.

Low standover height for improved crotch clearance

Heavy duty frame material

Wide and high riser bar for maximum control

Long travel rear suspension

Long travel fork for maximum shock absorbency

Large soft compound tyres – for extra traction and bump absorption

Disc brake with large rotor for greater stopping power

Platform pedals preferred by many riders

Single chainring with chain retention device

Many winter ski resorts are now allowing, indeed actively encouraging, mountain bikers to use their lifts in summer months. This is a bonus for riders with heavy-duty suspension laden specialist downhill bikes, and a bonus for resorts looking for tourist income out of the ski season.

The thrill of speed, the necessity for skill, the need for concentration, instant reaction to fast approaching obstacles, the ability of the bike's suspension and other technical attributes to deal with the abuse being handed out by the trail – they're all factors that conspire to create the adrenalin buzz that can only come with potentially risky activities. Of course, the real buzz comes from successfully dealing with the risk.

While anyone can score the downhill buzz on any bike and at any level of competence or confidence, there are bikes built just for downhill. Pure downhill bikes haven't really been a commercial success, because most of them are bought, often via low cost sponsorship deals, by racers who then proceed to wreck them in crash-filled competition practice. Hardly any specialist downhill bikes remain popular or current for more than a season or two, and those that you come across at bargain prices on the second-hand market will often have been subjected to almost terminal abuse. But downhill bikes have still been good for the industry because they've set the scene for hard hitting everyman all-rounder bikes.

Pure downhill machines are a specialist breed, not really suited to the sort of terrain where the forces of gravity are not in your favour. They will be designed to absorb big, often accidental, hits from the harshest rock-strewn terrain and that will often mean loads of extra weight and somewhere between 150 and 300mm of plush suspension travel, dialled in for damage limitation rather than pedalling efficiency.

There is no one frame or suspension design that typifies the specialist downhill bike. From a racer's point of view (most design is race led) it's a horses for courses thing. A 16kg (35lb) single pivot bike with about 120mm of fork travel and 150mm at the back may be perfect for some courses while others are best served by a 20kg (45lb) multi-linkage bike with 150mm of fork travel and 200mm at the back.

Just as bikes vary enormously, riders do too. Even among racers, there are some who can perform superbly on highly technical and super-steep courses on slimy surfaces, whereas others appear to need fitness-based courses with loads of traction. The real stars are capable of winning on any sort of course, and this is where natural ability, fast reflexes, full body fitness and thoughtful bike, tyre and componentry choices are just as crucial as pure nerve. Pay no attention to anyone who says downhill racing is a no-brainer thing. If that's your approach, you won't last long. The top downhill racers are a remarkably switched-on breed.

Air shocks are increasingly taking over from coil shocks, even on long travel bikes.

Freeride or All Mountain bikes range from heavy duty trail bikes to big drop/stunt bikes. Their essential attribute is that you can do almost anything on them.

Freeride/all mountain

With so few riders being able to maintain a long-term interest in riding a purist downhill bike, it was only a matter of time before go-anywhere do-anything bikes evolved. 'Freeride' is a tag that's emerged from other adrenaline-fuelled sports. It means all manner of things to all manner of rider types, but the basic notion is that Freeride bikes and their riders form a partnership with a 'can-do' attitude. If something looks vaguely rideable, it's worth trying. 'All Mountain' bikes, which often get confused with Freeride bikes, are at the lighter end of the Freeride spectrum, with a little more emphasis on go anywhere pedalling ability and a little less emphasis on going over big drops. All Mountain might even be referred to by some riders as 'Freeride Light'.

Saddle low on weight and adjustable for height

Frame reinforced but medium weight

Suspension fork long travel for bigger hits

Rear suspension allows reasonable climbing characteristics

Disc brake big rotors for high power stopping

Triple chainset Not strictly necessary but extra chainrings offer wider gear ratios for climbing

Freeride bikes are the choice for 'downhillers at heart'. They will carry you downhill almost as well as the specialist downhill bikes, but they can usually cope well with the uphills too. Pedalling efficiency is more crucial than on pure downhill bikes, so the frame and suspension design will usually be position and travel-adjustable to suit whatever terrain you choose to tackle. Most Freeride bikes will be fitted with a range of gears that can deal with extreme ups as well as downs.

Because riders look for climbing ability as well as big hit ability on Freeride bikes, weight saving is an issue. During the last few years, we have seen Freeride bikes diversify in design as much as mountain bikes in general. 'Freeride-Lite' has almost become a genre in itself and there is now a breed of hardtail (without rear suspension) bikes with longer travel forks that are referred to as 'Freeride-Hardtails'.

At the other end of the spectrum, there are many heavy-duty big hitting Freeride bikes aimed at riders who seek downhill thrills and adventure. These are the sort of riders who make for great magazine coverage, jumping off seemingly impossible drops, riding over and off all sorts of natural and man-made obstacles… basically seeking out, and often constructing, the sort of terrain that no 'ordinary' rider would go near. This sort of riding is often referred to as 'North Shore', after the radical terrain and imaginative log constructions found on Canada's Vancouver North Shore.

A super plush, heavy-duty, hard hitting, big obstacles Freeride bike might offer as much suspension travel as (occasionally more than) a downhill bike, and some pure stunt machines have been known to weigh 22kg (49lb) or more. But the more typical everyman Freeride bike will vary between a Freeride-Lite 14kg (31lb) with 100–120mm of suspension travel and a harder-hitting 17kg (38lb) with 120–150mm of travel.

As you can see, there is no Freeride norm. From a technical perspective, it's one of the fastest growing areas of mountain biking. Inevitably, the thoroughbred Freeride bikes are at the leading edge, as downhill bikes were a few years back, so they tend to cost a lot of money. But a trickle-down effect of leading edge technology is increasingly making room for reasonably priced Freeride styled bikes in lower price brackets.

In many ways, buying yourself a bike with a Freeride identity is more a fashion and attitude statement than anything. Few riders can push these bikes to their limits, just as few four-wheel-drive owners push their vehicles to the limits. But there's nothing wrong with buying the bike to suit your dreams and aspirations. While a Freeride bike may be a tad heavier to haul up hills than a 'normal' cross country full suspension bike, it will readily forgive rider error and can offer the sort of big hit ability that would probably damage a normal MTB. For many riders, the fun of riding lies here rather than in hill climbing speed.

Long travel single crown forks have now become more popular than twin crown forks for most thrill seeking riders.

Suspension design on cross country bikes means all your effort goes to the rear wheel and not into the rear shock.

Cross country full suspension

There was a time when every cross country mountain bike racer rode a lightweight fully rigid bike. It was only a decade ago that suspension forks started to prove their worth. Cross country racers took years to be convinced that the extra weight of a suspension fork was a burden worth accepting for the sake of the comfort, damage avoidance, control at speed and a big decrease in body punishment. As the forks got better, more and more riders started to use them. Now the same is happening with rear suspension. The designs have improved to a level where even the top cross country racers are often choosing to ride full suspension bikes. Inevitably, ordinary riders are too.

Saddle high for optimum power transfer

Suspension shorter travel design for small hits and climbing efficiency

Frame lightweight for fast acceleration and climbing

Bars flat and narrow but riser bars are becoming popular

Disc brakes or rim brakes for lower weight

Wheelset lightweight with minimalist tyre tread for speed

Actually, ordinary riders can gain more from a full suspension bike than the racers. Racers are a hardened bunch who don't mind putting up with discomfort and suffering. It's an assumption of racing. If it doesn't hurt you're not trying hard enough. The cross country racer's obsession with lightweight bikes comes from the fact that many races are won or lost on climbs. Even if a full suspension bike climbs well, as most of them do these days (either through pure design efficiency or through ability to lock-out the suspension), the extra weight of the frame and shock is still a minor disadvantage on smooth climbs. Minor speed disadvantages are no big deal to ordinary riders, but can be enough to cause a racer to lose contact with a climbing group.

Obviously, a well designed and well set up full suspension bike offers a big advantage as soon as the going gets rough. Its potential for speed on rough ground, its improved control and its extra comfort makes a small amount of extra weight worthwhile in most situations. There are times when a full suspension bike will tackle the rougher climbs better than a hardtail too. This is because good rear suspension designs produce the sort of boost in traction and control that allows you to pedal harder and carry your speed better.

Early efforts at cross country full suspension bikes were often flawed by misguided designs (usually poor main pivot placement) and excessive weight, not to mention dubious long-term durability. But weights came down and designs improved to a point where the oft' talked about 'pedal energy robbing' through the suspension motion became minimal enough to ignore. Any slight energy loss and weight gain must now be

weighed up against rider energy gain, and speed gain, through increased comfort, traction, confidence and control. There are loads of different ways to design an efficient cross country full suspension bike, and these days most designs are incredibly well executed. In fact many bikes, for those who still worry about pedal energy being robbed, offer instant lock-out capability on the rear shock, either on the shock itself or via a thumb shifter control on the handlebar.

A few studies have been carried out to try to work out how much energy and speed is won, or lost, by the best full suspension designs versus the best hardtail designs. The results are interesting but inconclusive. Race results speak louder. An increasing amount of racers are winning on full suspension bikes. It's a horses for courses thing. Some riders gain more than others on different types of terrain. But one thing is certain: cross country full suspension bikes are more comfortable and a lot more fun to ride than hardtails when the going gets rough.

Inevitably, there is some overlap between cross country full suspension and 'Freeride-Lite'. Most top-end cross country bikes are designed with race-level performance in mind, but manufacturers know that most of them are bought by riders who rarely, if ever, race. The most expensive cross country race-bred full suspension bikes might weigh as little as 10kg (22lb), but the more accessible middle of the range bikes are likely to weigh 12–13kg (27–29lb). Frame designs range from pivot free (the chainstays flex) 'Soft-tails' with under 50mm of travel, to the many and varied single pivot and four-bar linkage configurations with between 70mm and 120mm of travel. (See the Bike anatomy chapter for more details.)

A rocker activated shock unit on a medium travel full suspension bike.

Cross country hardtails

The cross country hardtail (front suspension only) is the 'traditional' cross country race bike. It was only about a decade ago that suspension forks made their mark, and since then they've slowly come to dominate the hardtail market, to a point where even budget priced cross country bikes are hard to find with a rigid fork. Of course, at the top end of the market, the hardtail is slowly but surely being out-gunned in the hype stakes by bikes with suspension at both ends. But many riders still love the relative purity of the lightweight hardtail. It's a very relevant speed option and it attracts riders at every price point.

The hardtail is the most versatile bike for just getting out there and having fun.

Saddle and post usually with a quick release for easy adjustment

Gears 24 or 27 speed, reliable and easy to use

Frame usually butted aluminium for low weight

Suspension fork short travel and low weight

Rim brake simple and lightweight

Tyres grippy, medium width and faster on the road too

With the average generic aluminium hardtail frame weighing well under 2kg (4.5lb) and the lightest weighing under 1.5kg (3.3lb) it's not at all surprising that weight-obsessed riders usually favour hardtails. The lightest suspension frames tip the scales at about 2.5kg (5.5lb), and most are far heavier. It would not be unusual to find a pro level racer riding a hardtail weighing less than 9.5kg (21lb), but average mid-range bikes still weigh 11.5kg (25.5lb) or so. It's the componentry that makes the difference. Expensive top-end componentry is nearly always quite a lot lighter than moderately priced mid-range stuff. For example, a pro race level cross country fork will often weigh half a kilogram less than a fork on a mid-range bike.

Low weight and ease of manufacture has meant that aluminium frames have come to dominate the hardtail market. Steel frames are usually a fair bit heavier (500g or so) than alu frames. They've fallen from favour over the last five years, but they still have their fans. A top steel frame has more 'feel' than a top aluminium frame. 'Feel' is hard to quantify, but there's no doubt that alu frames usually feel slightly harsher over bump strewn terrain. They rely more on bigger tyres and a well padded saddle for comfort. Titanium and carbon composite hardtail frames also offer a superb ride feel (like steel, titanium and carbon have more 'give' than alu) but they're costly. Tubular magnesium frames are gaining favour in some quarters, mainly because they offer a low-vibration ride feel, and they're very light, but it remains to be

seen whether magnesium will ever be fully accepted as a frame material.

We cover the finer points of hardtails in our Bike anatomy chapter, but it's the oft-stated 'purity' of a hardtail that will ensure its survival as full suspension bikes win out in the hype stakes. Many riders love the fact that a hardtail puts you more directly in contact with the terrain and your pedal power. Looking at this negatively, it means you feel the bumps more. Looking at it positively, it means you learn to ride with a level of grace and finesse that helps you to tame the terrain. Learn to ride off-road on a hardtail and you'll be a better rider in the long run.

Racers and leisure riders still predominantly choose no-nonsense bikes without rear suspension.

It's all about self expression and pushing your skill and body to the limit.

Mountain cross/dirt jump

As you can see from the inconclusive title, it's not easy to pigeon hole this bike type. Even Freeride is easier to quantify. Slalom, BSX (Bicycle Super Cross), Biker Cross, Mountain Cross, Dirt Jump – call it what you will, the bikes are essentially BMX attitude encompassed in a mountain bike. There are minor differences between the bikes for each discipline, but in essence one hardcore bike type can tackle all disciplines.

Chain device stops the chain from derailing

Wheels heavy duty for hard landings

Gears single chainring at the front and close ratio at the rear

Frame medium travel, hard hitting frame or tough and compact hardtail frame

Riser bar high position and reinforced for strength

Tyres fat and grippy with a soft compound

Some use clipless pedals for Mountain Cross but most prefer flats for stunt riding

Strength, in the frames, the forks and the componentry, is an overriding feature of these bikes. Everything needs to be capable of taking the sort of abuse that few other bikes suffer. The frames are very compact with thick walled tubes, boxed sections and lots of reinforcement features. Aluminium is the dominant build material these days, but steel actually makes a lot more sense and it seems likely that steel tubed frames will make a comeback in the near future. The forks, the wheels and the rest of the componentry are usually heavily built in order to withstand the inevitable crashes and bad landings. Even good landings might be enough to crisp wheels, crumple frames and snap handlebars on a normal bike.

Confusingly, all these disciplines feature both hardtail and suspension bikes, and there's no real consensus about frame geometry or gearing. Some riders (especially those who have grown up with BMX bikes) choose to ride a single gear on a rigid frame and fork, others choose a hardtail with a long travel suspension fork, others choose full suspension. Some bikes have 24 inch instead of 26 inch wheels and no one can decide whether the frames should be short or long in terms of reach.

The main thing that characterises these bikes is hardnut build quality, or simply hardnut imagery where some of the 'me-too' low budget jump bikes are concerned. The rider's preference for a low saddle, while not a very practical choice for getting to places, signifies readiness for the sort of radical manoeuvres that these

bikes are made for. Single ringed heavy-duty cranksets are the norm, usually with special guides to stop the chain from jumping off. Many of these bikes, at least the hardtail versions, can readily double up as urban playtime machines.

As with BMX, and downhill to an extent, many of these bikes are bought by riders who simply like the image and attitude that the bikes suggest. Among those who actually use and abuse the bikes to a level somewhere near what they're capable of, there's a wide array of styles and ability. Some riders just love to hang out at jump spots, without being able to achieve much more than a small bunny hop, while some perform stunts with the sort of style that would suggest circus training.

Jumping is a great skill to develop, and not just for showing off. It'll make you a better all-round rider.

There's no such thing as unridable. The only thing holding you back is your skill and imagination.

Trials bikes

A trials bike, not to be confused with a trail bike, is a bike that's been modified, or sometimes specially made, for riding (or hip-hopping) over challenging urban and rural obstacles. Obviously, you could have a go at trials on any bike, but there's a special breed of modified MTB that's not much good for anything else.

Saddle small and low to prevent interference

Frame compact and super strong to withstand high impacts

A rigid fork will often be preferred to suspension

Chainring tiny rock clearance and high torque

Tyres big, soft and grippy for maximum traction

Pedals large and grippy platform pedals for superior foot contact

Ten years ago MTB trials used to simply rely on an excellent sense of balance and control when riding over obstacles and difficult terrain at slow speed. There was a time in the UK when the national MTB champion was decided through combined points gained in cross country, downhill and trials. But gradually trials, like downhill and BSX/slalom, became a discipline in their own right. As riders became more expert at tackling an increasingly difficult range of obstacles, ride styles became dominated by hip-hopping and jumping from spot to spot, to the point where some sections could almost be completed on a bike without a chain.

Special trials MTBs usually have 26 inch wheels, but some use 24 inch. MTB trials are generally kept separate from 'traditional' 20 inch wheel trials, although inevitably there's some overlap because many riders are good at both. In theory, a standard MTB can be turned into a trials-ready MTB simply by dropping the saddle. Removing the big chainrings and fitting a bash-ring will give you more clearance and protection for hopping onto or over obstacles. Fitting much bigger tyres and/or running your tyres soft will give you more traction ... but watch out for pinch punctures. If you plan to attempt radical manoeuvres, put some thought into whether your frame, fork, wheels and componentry are really strong enough for the inevitable occasional impact with solid objects.

There are trials competitions for both MTB and 20 inch wheeled bikes. But equally, there are riders who simply want to hang out in town centres and play on street furniture. Steps, benches, walls, fountains,

fences, bollards, etc are all as enticing to urban trialsters as roots, rocks, twists, turns and drop-offs are to rural trailsters. Big drop and gap-jump stunts are best achieved with a nonchalance that implies total spontaneity rather than the reality of months of unseen practice, frequent failure and regular injury.

Trials riders break as many bikes as dirt jumpers or downhillers. Non-reinforced MTB frames will tend to break behind the head tube, half way along the top/down tube or near the bottom bracket. Steerers and head tubes bend when subjected to vicious impacts. Normal bottom bracket axles and cranks may snap. Unprotected chainrings bend. Bars and stems bend and snap. Wheels get tacoed. Tyres burst. In short, anything that's not specially made to take abuse will not last long in a trials situation.

Natural obstacles and street are tackled with equal gusto by the skilled trials rider.

Just riding along

Not to be underestimated, the JRA (Just Riding Along) bike is the bike that most people buy. It's the comfortable non-specialist machine that enables you to have a go at pretty much anything a bike can do, and still go shopping with panniers or a kiddie seat on the back.

The first and most popular choice for many first time mountain bikers and commuters.

Saddle cushioned for comfort

Tyres often semi-slick for great speed on the flats

Handlebars upright riding position

Gears simple and easy to use

Low cost componentry to keep the prices at the beginners' level

This is the bike that has made the Mountain Bike into a mainstream bike for every man, woman and child. It's the generic entry-level MTB, but it has also spawned all manner of off-shoots and sub-categories for those who really don't want, or need, a thoroughbred big tyred off-road bike. A JRA bike will range from a perfectly adequate suspension fork-equipped trail bike to something that just borrows aspects of MTB technology.

The Hybrid, the Adventure Bike, the Town and Country Bike, the Comfort Bike, the Sports Bike, the Recreation Bike – the sky's the limit as far as the number of marketing names is concerned. The thing they all have in common is that they've emerged because of the commercial success of the MTB, and most of them are built using predominantly MTB parts.

If there's one major factor that sets JRA MTBs apart from all other JRA bike categories, it's the tyres. While true MTBs will typically have big knobbly tyres fitted, the bike manufacturers have recognised that many people rarely ride off-road and are better served by a compromise tyre. Minimally treaded tyres with a fast rolling centre strip are better than heavy knobblies for road and dry gentle trail use. However, even if most of your riding is on Tarmac, try to resist the temptation to go for the skinny tyres that road racing bikes use. Unless you're a racer, you'll be far better

served by the extra comfort, shock absorption and consequent damage limitation of big profile tyres. Provided you keep them inflated to recommended pressures, they'll roll almost as well as skinnies too.

Maximum adjustability and adaptability is the key to the ideal JRA bike, especially as these are the bikes that are often shared between riders with different needs and body shapes. Not everyone wants a handlebar, stem and saddle in the same position, so look for long seat posts, front and rear saddle rail adjustment and height adjustment in stems. When a stem bolts straight on to the steerer (the Aheadset system), look out for washers on the top of the fork steerer. These can be placed over or under the stem for height adjustment. Also check for luggage rack and mudguard eyelets, ideally ready-threaded for firmer fixing. For off-road use, full length mudguards might attract unwanted twigs and mud, but for urban riding they make a lot of sense, as does a luggage rack.

Most entry-level MTBs are now fitted with a suspension fork. If you're looking for a bike for urban use only, try to find one of the few with a rigid fork. Suspension might offer a little more comfort and damage limitation on potholed urban streets, but you'd be better off saving a bit of weight and money and investing in more suitable tyres, mudguards, a good lock and a rack.

Inexpensive simple bikes for inexpensive simple pleasures.

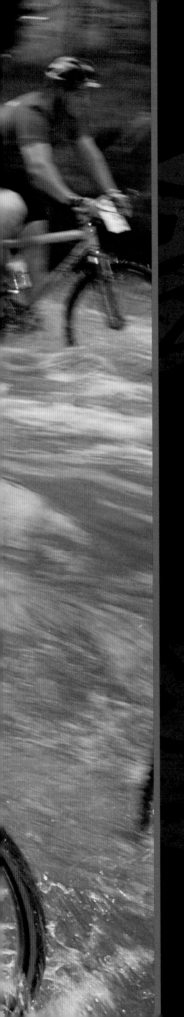

CHAPTER 3

Competitive urges

Some people just love to compete, and mountain biking offers almost as many competitive disciplines as athletics. From the skills, thrills and spills of downhill racing (which is where it all started), to the mind-numbing toughness of a long distance epic, to the hop, skip and jump of competitive trials – whatever discipline you happen to be good at on the many mountain bike types described in our previous chapter, there is bound to be an organised competitive element on offer.

Cross country racing (main picture) is currently the only MTB discipline to qualify as an Olympic sport, but there are loads of others such as trials (left), slalom (right) and enduro racing which are hotly contested at international as well as national level. Even at a regional level you can bet that there's an MTB event on this weekend somewhere near you...

Downhill racing

If you subscribe to the conventional telling of mountain bike history, mountain bikes were invented by a bunch of guys racing converted beach cruisers down mountain fire roads in California (read Chapter One for the full story). There's a strong argument, therefore, for downhill racing as the original form of mountain bike competition. Today, while the sport of mountain biking has diversified and spread, downhill racing is still the highest profile branch.

'Downhill racing is a big adrenalin sport. Reaching speeds of up to 60mph on off-road tracks has got to give you a buzz – hitting jumps and flying through the air is a great feeling...' So says Steve Peat, Yorkshireman and 2002 UCI Downhill World Cup Champion. He started riding bikes for fun and now he's the best in the world.

Downhill racing used to be no more complex than simply riding from the top of a mountain to the bottom as fast as possible. Today courses are a mix of natural terrain and hand-crafted trail features such as berms and jumps for increased speed, style and spectator thrills.

It's easy to see why. At the top level downhill racing is incredibly fast and close, with races often being settled by gaps of tiny fractions of a second. The downhill World Cup circuit takes in events all over the world, with teams travelling between them with big box vans and all the paraphernalia of a global sport. Economic pressures over recent years have seen a fair amount of downsizing, with some teams disappearing altogether, but the spectacle remains undiluted.

A world class downhill course is a serious test of rider ability. An ordinary recreational rider would struggle to make it down the course in one piece, let alone be in a position to try and do it fast. As suspension and brake technology have progressed, so downhill courses have developed, becoming bigger, steeper, rougher, and faster. World level courses have reached the point where a big-travel downhill bike doesn't merely give you an advantage, it's a prerequisite to completing the course. When you consider that a top-notch DH bike packs up to nine inches of suspension travel, you get some idea of just how extreme some of the race courses are.

There's not really any such thing as a 'typical' downhill track. Course designers put a lot of effort into making their run distinctive from the rest, and every course has its own character. To become World Cup champion you have to be able to perform on a wide variety of different styles of course, from flat-out, high speed power courses to tight and technical skill courses and all points in between.

Some courses require an ability to pedal flat out for seven minutes and control a bike at speeds in excess of 50mph. And no matter how smooth and open a course may appear from trackside, at 50mph on a bike bumps get magnified and corners arrive very quickly... At the other extreme are courses where large stretches are negotiated at no more than jogging speed, but over rock steps, oblique roots and trails so steep that walking down them would be a challenge.

The racers' favourite courses, though, are those that combine these disparate elements into one run. A course that has riders sprinting full bore across an open mountainside one minute and then heaving on the brakes for a plunge through twisty, tree-lined trails the next is the ultimate test of a rider's strength, bike handling skill, bravery and reactions.

For there's a great deal more to downhill racing than just pointing the bike downhill and holding on. Downhillers have often been accused of being fearless but unthinking. But to win, you have to think. Races are won by the riders who make the fewest mistakes, and you don't put in a flawless run by leaving your brain in the start hut. The sheer volume of information that has to be processed by a downhill racer is staggering. To be successful they have to deal not just with corners, berms and jumps but roots, rocks, drops, off-camber sections, loose or slippery trail surfaces and dozens of other things that could all make the difference between winning and losing. And that's before the ever-growing influence of strategy across races in a series, such as deliberately qualifying with a slow time to get an early run to avoid a change in the weather...

But despite the incredible difficulty of downhill racing at the top level, it's still a very accessible sport at local and even national level. Most domestic courses are ridable even on a hardtail bike. You're unlikely to win thus equipped but you can get a flavour of things. And if the downhill bug takes hold, the sport is possibly unique in that you can buy pretty much everything that the pros use off the shelf.

We'll give Steve Peat the last word: 'If you get into racing then you will have fun, whether you're riding with your friends in your local woods or if you go racing, the fun is always there. This is my tenth year racing and it's still fun to me. Every race is a new challenge and I love winning – standing on the podium with a bottle of champagne and hearing the cork pop is the best feeling in the world.'

Downhill racing is a solo game – the rider vs the clock. Some World Cup courses take as little as 5 minutes to complete, with riders pushing speeds of up to 60mph in sections.

Cross country racing

For many years cross country (or XC) racing was the mainstay of competitive mountain biking. Almost as soon as those pioneering Californians had bodged multiple gears on to their beach cruisers to allow them to ride back up the hills they'd just raced down (rather than chucking all the bikes in the back of a truck) it occurred to them to race the bikes up the hills too. And thus cross country racing was born.

'The difference between MTB racing and other cycle sport is that in mountain biking you can compete against the circuit as well as against other riders. If you don't win you can still be satisfied that you've finished a demanding and technical race.' Oli Beckingsale is twice British National XC Champion. It's easy to say it's not all about winning when you win all the time, but when it comes to cross country mountain bike racing he has a sound point.

In a parallel strand of MTB development, riders from Crested Butte in Colorado were holding an annual event, the Pearl Pass Tour. It involved attempting to ride (and usually pushing) up the eponymous pass before descending into Aspen and back. The Tour had faded before being revived by the attendance of the Marin pioneers on their newly geared bikes.

Many of the new breed of mountain bikers were fit road racers, so it was no surprise that a form of racing that placed as much importance on strength and fitness as skill and bravery flourished. And early XC races certainly stressed strength and fitness, being usually point-to-point or single-lap affairs of epic extent. Fifty mile single-lap races weren't uncommon in the early years of mountain biking.

The needs of spectators and the difficulties of running races over such wide areas of countryside led to most cross country racing developing into a multi-lap format over a shorter course, typically four or five miles. This arrangement also allowed races to be held for a number of categories simply by making more experienced racers ride more laps. Race categories were developed, with younger riders racing against others in their age group and adult riders split up along skill and experience lines from Sport to Elite.

Not that things were quite that formalised for a while. The organisers of early mountain bike races of all forms were very much winging it, with a vague course in mind, a meeting point in a pub and results often determined by who could remember being in front of whom at the end. Occasionally the race wouldn't even be run – according to MTB legend, the winner of the 1988 British National Championships was decided by a majority vote in the pub, the weather being too bad to race!

Over the years, though, things became more and more professional. And today XC is the only form of mountain bike competition to be an Olympic sport. Cross country is the most purely athletic type of MTB racing. Sure, bike handling skill, bravery and tactics all play an important part, but in cross country strength and stamina are what win races.

Unfortunately, XC became a victim of its own professionalism. As the racers got faster and fitter and the bikes got lighter and more single-minded, so courses began to move away from technical challenge. Increasing numbers of riders crossing over from road racing and starting to apply road racing tactics compounded matters. Gradually the courses got smoother, faster, easier to ride, more of a race track. And as the technical challenge diminished, so did the grass-roots appeal. With less interesting courses, riders racing for fun dwindled and XC became increasingly elitist.

But traditional XC won't go away. It's still the best test of a rider's all-round ability. You have to be able to climb as well as you can drop, be at

home spinning gears in a pack and ducking and dodging tree roots, be able to ride for upwards of two hours without blowing but keeping back a sprint for the end. No other race format demands such a breadth of ability. And with many ex-racers having been attracted back into racing by enduro and marathon events there's signs of a groundswell back towards good old cross country racing. Take it from Oli:

'The reason I started racing was that I liked having an event to aim for. I enjoyed the racing because I could get stuck in, give it everything, try and beat my mates and then talk about it for hours. Boring everyone with my stories on the crash, the sprint or whatever.'

Cross country racing is still the best test of a rider's all-round ability demanding great bike handling and fitness, stamina, determination and speed.

Mountain cross

The original mountain bike race formats, cross country and downhill, tended to involve sizeable courses spread out over a wide area. For a fledgling action sport trying to get noticed by TV, this wasn't ideal. What was needed was a more compact, tighter, faster form of racing, preferably with lots of potential for crashes. So slalom racing was born.

'BSX is something that anyone from the inner to the seasoned pro can get addicted to. The challenge of overcoming your fears to jump a double that may be the biggest you have ever tried – but if you want to win you know you're gonna have to do it.' Scott Beaumont is a past BMX World Champ and a BSX/dual mountain bike racer. And if he's talking about overcoming fears you know you're dealing with a potentially scary sport.

The first slalom courses were simply a sloping field with ski slalom poles stuck in to create two approximately equal lanes. This format became known as dual slalom. Two riders went head-to-head, each pair racing twice and swapping lanes to even up potential lane advantages. Since then, just like mountain biking as a whole, slalom has developed and diversified. Courses became steeper and sprouted bermed corners and jumps. But they retained two lanes, until the development of 'duel' slalom. In this format there are two start lanes but no requirement to stay in one lane all the way down. Often there's only one fast line, resulting in both riders trying to elbow each other out of the way to get on it. It's a fast, exciting event with as many crashes as you'd expect.

Slalom development didn't stop there. The next stage was more riders, with four or even six competitors racing on the same course. The multiple rider format is commonly known as BSX (for Bicycle Super Cross). It's effectively BMX racing on steroids, with bigger bikes, bigger courses that run downhill, and enormous jumps. You'll see effectively the same set-up going by a number of different names according to who the race promoter/sponsor is. Biker Cross (or Biker-X), 4X, quad slalom, mountain cross – they're all essentially the same thing. Some courses are longer than others, with some events taking place on courses that would do a downhill race proud. The common elements, though, are the built nature of the course. Downhill courses tend to make use of naturally occurring features. If a BSX course builder wants something in his course he'll get a digger and a few tons of dirt and put it where he wants it.

Building a course has become an art form. The designer crafts all the jumps, berms and lines to guide riders where he wants them to go for the maximum action potential.

It takes a particular kind of rider to excel at BSX. Aggression, power and bike handling ability are paramount. Races can be won and lost out of the start gate – there's a huge advantage in hitting the first berm or jump out in front. But cunning design means that BSX races are rarely a foregone conclusion and it's always possible for the skilled rider to work the course in his favour to get ahead from an apparently losing position. Often the passing move involves the leader taking a tumble, but that's all in a day's work. Indeed, the potential for injury in BSX is sufficiently high that, while most downhill racers take part in BSX events, several refuse to (or their sponsors forbid them) on the grounds that a BSX injury could ruin their chances in what they see as the main event, the downhill.

This often leaves the field open to the BSX specialists. Unsurprisingly, ex-BMX racers are often the riders to beat. The short, fast nature of the races is almost exactly akin to BMX, with BMX riders having only to get used to the higher speeds, bikes with gears (although some run just one anyway) and wider choice of lines. Riders coming from downhill have to learn fast starts and paying attention to other riders on the course. But it's possible to win coming from either end of the spectrum.

Scott Beaumont again: 'BSX is the most technical part of mountain bike sport. The fitness, mental strength, skill and balls needed to succeed is greater than in any other branch of the sport. The twist is that even if you have all these attributes, there's no guarantee that you'll ever win – full contact is allowed and you can be taken out at any time.'

Bicycle Super Cross (BSX) is the ultimate MTB spectator event. Courses are short but speed, bike showmanship and danger is the name of the game as up to four riders battle their way to the finish line.

Dirt jumping

There's a degree of confusion over the meaning of the word 'trails'. To the cross country rider or freerider, a trail is a path that actually goes somewhere. To the dirt jumper, a trail is a sequence of jumps linked together. 'Riding trails' is used to distinguish dirt jumping from street riding or skate park riding. Riders will typically invest huge amounts of time building their trails, and not surprisingly they have a strong sense of ownership that can often manifest itself as hostile territorialism.

'Dirt Jumping is all about self expression and pushing yourself beyond your comfort zone.' So says dirt jumper Grant 'Chopper' Fielder. As he demonstrates, dirt jumpers are people of few words. They'd rather let their riding do the talking. Which makes a lot of sense. In dirt jumping, it's not about being fastest, first or even highest or longest. It's about personal expression, about riding the trails with whatever you consider to be style. For some riders that just means smooth, for some it means big, for others it means tricks. The common thread is riding in the way you want and not being bothered about what other people are doing.

It is perhaps understandable. The attraction of dirt jumping for many riders lies at least as much in the building of the jumps as in the riding of them. Indeed, there are many devotees who spend more time digging than riding. They'll spend weeks sorting out drainage, shifting dirt, shaping the lips of the jumps to perfection, laying things out to permit transfers from one set of jumps to another… If someone comes along after all that work, comes up short on all the jumps and wrecks them, the creators are inevitably going to get upset.

The longest-lasting and most extravagantly developed jump spots are often hidden away in patches of woodland where no one else ever goes. Landowners have an (often unjustified) reputation for a total lack of understanding of the wishes of jump-building mountain bikers, and as jumps are often built without permission, they are under constant threat of being destroyed.

It's perhaps this strong sense of ownership and desire to protect the jumps themselves that leads to dirt jumpers tending to shun public exposure. All forms of mountain biking are essentially about doing, rather than being seen to be doing, but dirt jumping has the strongest underground ethos. Most riders actively avoid drawing attention to themselves, preferring to ride with a small, close-knit group. The competitive element usually means trying to pull a jump that you can't do yet, competing with yourself to improve.

That's not to say there's no such thing as a dirt jumping competition. Comps are a regular attraction at BSX and dual events and occasionally occur as standalone entities. But again, they're as much for the riders as for the spectators.

The whole scene is strongly linked to BMX. Many of the riders either used to ride BMX or still do. And in the same way that BMX dirt jumping and BMX racing are very different facets of what initially looks like the same sport, so BSX racing has a great deal in common with dirt jumping but paradoxically couldn't be more different.

Both activities involve sequences of jumps, but while the aim of BSX is to be fastest and get to the bottom of the hill first, the aim of dirt jumping is simply riding the jumps in whatever way feels the best to you. For even with dirt jumping there are different philosophies. Tricks win comps, so riders who do tricks are seen as 'sell-outs' by the hardcore jumpers for whom smoothness is everything and 'keeping it real' a priority. Conversely the tricksters see the 'core' riders as rather old-fashioned and self-important.

But what all the dirt jump sub-tribes have in common is that for them, the mountain bike isn't a tool for getting somewhere fast or covering distance. Instead it's a gymnastic device, at home in the air, ready and waiting to thumb its nose at gravity, flowing with the rider in a celebration of bike handling ability.

Influenced by BMX, dirt jumping tests rider skill and style to the limits as competitors pull huge aerial tricks over a variety of jumps.

Trials

Most areas of mountain bike competition hinge on speed. They're usually a question of who can cover the distance in the least time. Observed trials, to give it its full name, is different. Bike racing assumes that actually getting around the course isn't too hard. The difficulty lies in doing it quickly. But trials makes no such assumptions. The challenge is simply to negotiate the course without putting your feet down or falling over.

'The appeal of trials is knowing that there are new things to learn on your bike all the time. The level is always rising and that keeps everything interesting. Competition trials is 10 per cent riding, 90 per cent mental, and that's no exaggeration. Being able to pull a ride out of the bag when it counts is a difficult thing to do, when you pull it off, it feels great. When you don't it hurts like hell.' Martyn Ashton has been trials World Champion and is one of the best known riders in the world. So he should know.

Trials riders display exceptional bike skills, and are happy hopping onto and over anything Mother Earth throws up at them or completing a specific course at a trials competition.

It sounds simple, and conceptually it is. But the practicalities of riding the course are far from simple. Trials events are held over a number of sections, none of which look immediately as if you could ride a bike over them. Rocks, logs and steep banks are common ingredients of traditional trials comps, and riders use a variety of techniques to negotiate them. At first glance, it doesn't appear to have a lot in common with riding a bike in the conventional sense.

Modern trials technique relies on spending a lot of time on the back wheel with the rear brake locked, hopping the bike across gaps or off drops. Indeed, such is the prevalence of the back-wheel riding style that competition trials bikes have extra strong back wheels, superlight front wheels and a riding position that only makes sense if the front wheel is a couple of feet higher than the back.

The other unique characteristic of trials is its unusual gestation. Bicycle trials has been a hugely popular sport in mainland Europe for many years, starting as an offshoot of motorcycles trials but quickly evolving into a sport in its own right. This branch of trials was focused on specialist trials bikes with 20 inch wheels. In the UK mountain bike trials grew from riders' desire to tackle ever more challenging terrain. Soon trials competitions were happening alongside conventional MTB races. Riders began to specialise and eventually the competitive side of MTB trials merged with the existing world of bicycle trials – trials comps today generally run two classes, 20 inch and 26 inch, in parallel.

This sequence of developments has resulted in two distinct trials cultures. Competition trials is, naturally, all about competition. They're almost always held out in the countryside, in woods with lots of logs, stumps and banks or out on the moors with rock outcrops and boulders. Competition bikes are lightweight and demand a smooth riding style. The emphasis in competitions is completing the course and making the fewest mistakes. There are no prizes for showing off.

The other culture is the sizeable recreational trials movement. Most riders aren't interested in competitions, or not formal ones. If there's any element of competition it's between riders and obstacles, as they constantly strive to land bigger drops, get up higher obstacles and clear wider gaps, all driven by informal rivalry between friends. This wing of trials often takes place in urban areas – many of the riders are young, their only form of transport is their bike and a trials bike doesn't lend itself to covering large distances, so they ride near home – and there's a growing influence of street BMX riding.

Needless to say, 'street' trials can be very hard on bikes. The terrain is unforgiving, and the riders' quest to always go a bit bigger inevitably leads to crashes. Trials bikes not intended for competition are therefore necessarily a little bit beefier and heavier. But this merely serves to make them more capable in the

hands of a skilled rider. Without worries about the equipment letting them down, riders can experiment more, finding new boundaries and extending the limits of what's possible on a bike.

Straddling the worlds of competition and recreation is the thriving demo scene. Even to non-mountain bikers, a trials display at an outdoor event or even in a shopping centre always draws a crowd. Most people are familiar with what bicycles are meant to be able to do, and trials falls well outside those parameters. Doing demos is one of the few ways to earn a living as a trials rider, and while good demo riders are always potent challengers in competition, there's a degree of showmanship necessary in demos that not all riders have. It's not enough to be able to ride brilliantly, you have to be able to work the crowd, get them excited, get them wanting more.

As Martyn Ashton says, 'The demo side can be fun but it is hard to make shows work. There are a lot of variables that contribute to a good demo. All I know is that if they start throwing fruit and veg it's time to stop.'

Marathon/Enduro

While conventional cross country racing was for many years the most popular form of MTB competition, the XC star has recently started to fade. A perception of increasing professionalism and focus on results put off riders who just wanted to 'have a go' and take part in an event for its own sake. Most people won't win, but when winning starts to look like the only appeal, people go elsewhere.

'Endurance events and in particular marathon type mountain bike events enjoy huge popularity in the UK based on their relaxed and friendly atmosphere. Riders are looking for the next big challenge but they similarly enjoy the camaraderie out on course and the festival like set-up which allows them to have a "proper" weekend away. Events offer a huge choice of courses and levels of difficulty which gives everybody the chance to find the right course for their ability...and even if something goes wrong out there, there are always medics, service stations and support crew at hand to get the riders home safely.' Mike Wilkens, UK Endurance event organiser.

Where they've gone to appears to be 'enduro' events. It's a term pinched from the world of off-road motorcycling, and it describes long events where the emphasis is as much on covering distance as on speed. It's an appropriate term. There are a few strands that weave together into the enduro umbrella. The simplest format is simply XC bike racing, but longer. One day events often have courses of 100km in length, a serious undertaking off-road. Big single-lap races are starting to happen all over the world. But on mainland Europe they've been doing it for years.

Races like the Roc d'Azur in France, the Crystalp in Switzerland and the Finnmarksturen in Sweden attract literally thousands of entrants. They're attracted not by the lure of a podium place, but by the sheer sense of occasion and achievement in taking part in and completing an epic ride. Big single-lap races share many of the same attractions as big all-day rides. They're usually in impressive settings, you get to see a lot of countryside without repeating your tracks and at the end you get a glow of satisfaction from having made it. The difference is that someone else works out the route for you and there are masses of other riders doing it at the same time. Extending the concept further, events like the TransAlp and the Trans Rockies are effectively MTB stage races, with a point-to-point course covered over a number of days.

Other enduro-style events involve warping the modern cross country race concept by keeping the relatively short course and multiple laps but hugely extending the time. The best known are 24-hour races. As with so many things in mountain biking, these were pioneered in the US but have been brought to Europe, and in particular to the UK, with amazing success. The original 24-hour format calls for teams of four or five riding relays, but a solo category for people who apparently have no concept of pain is a common feature.

The joy of 24-hour races is down to several factors. If you're racing as a team, it's a very social form of racing, especially as only one of you is racing at a time. And most riders don't usually ride at night, let alone race, so riding in darkness is something of a novelty. It's a unique experience racing through woodland with only lights on your handlebars to guide you. Many 24-hour race enthusiasts cite the night laps as the thing that keeps them coming back year after year.

The popularity of night-time racing has even led to races that do away with the daylight hours altogether, starting at dusk and racing through the night until dawn. There's also a host of races in shorter eight- or six-hour formats, usually for solo competitors. On the face of it, a six-hour solo race ought to be no harder than a 24-hour race in a team of four, but the longer format is actually easier as you may only be racing for an hour at a time, rather than having to do the whole lot in one hit.

The appeal of all these flavours of enduro is largely the same. Unlike conventional racing, there's sufficient challenge involved in merely completing the course that getting to the finish is an achievement. And as the enduro scene is a relatively new one, it's still got that sense of fun that many people feel has been lost from the traditional XC race. It may seem unlikely, but lots of people have made a 24-hour race their first ever bike race. It looks like going in at the deep end, but really a 24-hour race is not all that dissimilar to going away riding for the weekend with some mates. Enduro events are far closer in spirit to the sort of riding that most mountain bikers do.

The fact that getting to the finish is an achievement makes the races a whole lot more accessible. Most people can't realistically aspire to winning races, but everyone can aspire to finishing an epic enduro. John Stamstad again: 'I think the real attraction to long distance racing is the fact that there is more to it than winning or losing. Just finishing is an amazing goal.'

Enduro and Marathon events are unlimited in format. All day and all night events, solo and team, are common, as are multi-day events like the Trans Rockies in Canada and the Trans Wales in the UK.

Freeride

Freeriding is now an end unto itself rather than merely an entertaining sideshow to the main attraction. And developments in bike technology mean that the threshold of doable has moved to incredible new heights. Things that would have been impossible to ride a few years ago are now within the reach of the skilled rider with the right bike.

'For me Freeride is about getting away from it all and riding natural terrain in a creative way with your own style. I love the adrenalin rush, the buzz that comes with stepping outside your comfort zone, pushing yourself and seeing what you are really capable of. Making that drop, gap or jump is a great feeling. It spurs me on to push even harder the next time out.' So says Chris Smith, one of the group of Britain's top freeriders defining a new wave of mountain biking. In many ways, the current freeride craze is just an extension of the long and honourable tradition of attempting to ride things that you're not sure whether you can ride. This has always been a part of recreational mountain biking. Someone will spot something that looks like it might be 'doable' and, like as not, someone will step up to prove the point one way or the other.

There are a few strands to freeride, but one of the defining movements is centred on the North Shore of Vancouver, Canada. Often-marshy trail conditions led to local riders starting to build boardwalks on trails to traverse the worst bits. It wasn't long before the boardwalks became more elaborate and ceased to be merely there to avoid some soft bits of ground. Soon the boardwalks were the whole point of the ride. Rather than being put in to make things easier they sprang up to make things deliberately more challenging.

Log rides, see-saws and wooden bridges are all common elements on the North Shore. Riders regularly negotiate inches-wide constructions 15 feet above the forest floor. And at the end? Sometimes there will be a steep ramp back to terra firma, but often there's nothing at all – you just have to pull the front wheel up, pedal off the edge and hold on…

The act of riding off drops has become known as 'hucking', and it's a defining term of the modern freeride movement. Being able to ride narrow, steep, insanely technical trails is one thing, but if you want to make a name for yourself in the freeride world, you need to get in the videos. And the best way into the videos is to huck massive drops.

This is the area where bike technology has made the biggest impact. A bike with upwards of seven inches of rear suspension travel expands the horizons of ridable drops. King of the huck, Nevada's Josh Bender, is riding 40-feet-high cliff drops on a bike with 12 inches of travel. This, though, is at the far extreme of freeride. Bender's cliff weapon isn't really a freeride bike. It's a piece of highly specialist equipment, designed to do one job. Most riders like to maintain a healthy degree of versatility, and this is reflected in the versatility of the bikes.

A good freeride bike needs to pack the travel to take the sting out of big drops, while at the same time being nimble enough for technical and tight trails, strong enough to hold together, and light enough to go up and along hills. For freeride encompasses up and along as well as down. The emphasis is on riding places that you can't get to any other way than by bike. Freeride is a kind of extreme adventure riding – you'll get out to somewhere new and unexplored under your own steam, find some crazy thing to ride and ride it, ideally staying in one piece.

Freeride encompasses up and along as well as down, the emphasis is on riding places that you can't get to any other way than by bike.

Trailquest

If racing over a set course isn't your bag, you might well be interested in the genre of competitions that we'll call navigation events. Unlike a regular bike race, which involves covering a fixed course in the shortest time, most navigation events fix the time and leave the route up to the competitors. Points are gained by visiting checkpoints and punching your score card. Checkpoints that are distant, up steep hills or otherwise difficult to reach carry more points.

'The first events were full of bearded weirdies and even stranger bikes and women. The locations for the events were wild. Mountain bikers had never really been sent out to such places with only the gear in their rucksacks to survive a whole weekend out in the wind and rain, and often in the sleet, snow and frost.' Polaris veteran (and multiple winner) Gary Tompsett has been involved in the Polaris challenge since the beginning. So what's this UK centred endurance riding phenomenon all about?

The granddaddy of them all is the Polaris Challenge. Polaris events take place over two days, with seven hours riding on Saturday and five hours on Sunday. Competitors have to carry all the equipment they'll need – the location of the campsite isn't revealed until after the start, along with the list of which checkpoints are active and how many points they carry. You collect as many points as you can, biggest number of points wins. The appeal is far broader than round-the-fields bike racing. No matter how far down the results you finish, you've achieved something.

The emphasis is very much on personal challenges and having a good time. Indeed, founders of the Polaris Challenge, Roger Dillon, Graham Longstaff and Andrew Denton, developed the format as 'an antidote to circuit racing'. It's been a huge success. The first 1991 event attracted 400 riders. Now the Polaris happens three times a year with 1,000 or so riders at each. When you've done it once you're likely to keep returning.

Clearly, just being a bit good at riding a bike isn't enough to succeed at a Polaris. Map reading, navigation and route planning are all key skills. Teamwork and communication are vital – it's not just you, you've got a team-mate too. The Polaris rules state that you must stick together. Without wishing to over-dramatise things, a certain degree of mental toughness is usually required. There will probably come a point where you're cold, tired, a long way from the campsite and confused as to what to do next. This is not a good time to start bickering with your buddy. It's well worth teaming up with someone that you trust and get on with. You'll be sharing a small tent for a start…

A lot of people choose the summer event as their first Polaris – the weather's generally better and the format is tweaked slightly, placing the campsite back at the start/finish area and letting teams leave their tents pitched there, reducing the amount of kit they have to carry. But still, you might feel that the Polaris is a bit keen for a first foray into MTB orienteering-style events. Fortunately there are a number of less demanding but no less challenging events.

Trailquests are probably the best known. These follow essentially the same format except that they're held on a single day. Events are run by clubs affiliated to the Trail Cyclists Association and are between two and seven hours in length. Again, competitors must gather as many points as they can by visiting checkpoints. Trailquests have a solo category, and several events have a Youth category too, for competitors of the ages of 15 and 16. With less time to visit checkpoints, quick thinking and navigational accuracy are paramount. The beauty of the events is their accessibility. With such a range of categories pretty much anyone can take part. Choose an event of a suitable length, brush up your map reading skills and go for it.

If the Polaris Challenge is a marathon and Trailquests are the middle distance events, then MTBO is a sprint. Mountain Bike Orienteering isn't just a catch-all term for events involving bikes and checkpoints. It describes shorter, faster events,

more like traditional orienteering in style. While some MTBO events are 'Score' events, requiring competitors to amass points in a given time as with Polaris and Trailquest, most are 'Time' events. Competitors must visit checkpoints in a designated order, although the route they take between each is up to them. The fastest time wins. MTBO is the most overtly competitive member of the family, with great emphasis on speed. It's a fast-growing sport, driven primarily by foot orienteering clubs like EBOR. There's even an MTBO World Cup, with a World Championship.

The other piece of the MTB orienteering-style event jigsaw is made up of independently organised events, often in a shorter, more relaxed format. The Fat Tyre Challenges run by Trailbreak in the UK are two or three-and-a-half hour events, with the unique innovation of evening events in the dark as an extra-adventure option.

All of the different interpretations of the bike orienteering concept are hugely popular, and deservedly so. There's a competitive element but no pressure to take things seriously. There's a sense of adventure and of achievement and there's real camaraderie between competitors. Many lasting friendships form over a mug of tea in the Polaris campsite.

It's an addictive game. Gary Tompsett: 'Imagine having only ridden in your home county, entering an exciting new event miles away, and riding for a full 12 hours over totally new terrain. Then, imagine doing that two or three times a year, each time in a completely different part of the country. What better way of discovering MTB Britain can you possibly imagine?'

Navigation events require good team work, map reading, route planning and communication skills as well as bike handling. Events often take place over two days too so you have to carry around enough provisions, camping and bike repair equipment to see you through.

CHAPTER 4

Mountain bike fitness

There are no two ways about it. Mountain biking gets you fit, both mentally and physically. You'll enjoy your riding more if you get even fitter and, although we'll admit to being slightly biased, mountain biking is definitely one of the best ways to make yourself happier and healthier. In this chapter we'll talk you through everything you need to know about how your body works when you're biking. We'll tell you how to look after it and how to tune it to make yourself into the perfect mountain biking engine.

You don't need expensive kit to get fit, even a basic cycle computer will display your speed and distance covered so you can monitor your progress.

For professional MTBers like UK World Cup Champ Steve Peat, being number 1 is only 20% inspiration and 80% dedication.

The anatomy of fitness

As hard as you want...

The mountain bike gives you the ultimate breadth of exercise intensity. Whether you're pottering along a cycle path at walking pace or leading the head of the pack in a multi-stage race around the Alps, biking can be as hard or as easy as you want. It will protect your knees and body from the pounding that running and walking inflict, and it'll even let you roll along and rest a while on the downhills.

Biking can also be as relaxing or as racey as you want. Tackle the trails solo at your own pace with as many scenic stops as possible, or line up alongside a whole herd of panting maniacs trying to rip each other's legs off. The choice is entirely yours.

Above; Biking can be as hard or as relaxing as you want – tackle the trails at your own pace.

Main image; Pedalling a bike is miles more fun and kinder to your body than running, yet uses the same muscle groups.

Whether on-road or off, take time to soak up your surroundings and enjoy the ride, treating your lungs to as much fresh air as possible – it's free and you won't find it in any gym!

Wherever you want...

While everyone has their idea of the perfect mountain biking route, the truth is that you can ride almost everywhere, from the road outside to the woods round the corner to the ends of the earth. You don't need a pool or a gym or a river to row on, just saddle up and go. The mountain bike can also take you to the most beautiful and secluded spots faster and more silently than any other way of travelling. When you're on your bike you really are right in the natural elements, rather than watching it through a window.

Fresh air

By giving you the power to leave traffic far behind, mountain biking lets you open up your lungs and gulp down as much fresh air as possible. No air conditioning, no smog, no 30 other gasping classmates in an aerobics studio, just pure countryside air.

Cardiovascular fitness

The action of cycling not only charges your body with air, it also tunes your body to make maximum use of it. Cycling will improve your lung power, strengthen your heart, make the muscles it powers stronger and more efficient and greatly increase your body's ability to deal with all the stresses it faces. Whether those stresses are related to the general strain of living or to specific illness in later life, biking now will give you a better quality of life for the rest of your years.

All round strength

Mountain biking also has specific conditioning advantages over similar cardiovascular sports like road cycling and running. The constant work needed to control your bike over rough ground makes it a great all round conditioning exercise for your back, belly, shoulders, neck and arms.

The drugs do work

If the powers that be knew how good mountain biking can make us feel, they'd probably ban it. Adrenalin is a great stimulant for getting the maximum performance out of your body. However hard you think you can push yourself, that extra fizz and rush of your body's very own natural riding crop as you tackle a do-or-die moment releases energy and determination you never knew you had. Adrenalin's partner in crime, Endorphin, will also come coursing through your veins. While the adrenalin ebbs and the heart rate drops, Endorphins will flood you with a vivid burst of euphoria to chase away pain and leave you standing at the summit dripping with a sense of vibrant self achievement.

Mental stimulation

Because of the environment you're 'working' in, mountain biking makes exertion seem as easy as possible. Rather than forcing your body along another 100 virtual metres on a treadmill gym like some hapless human hamster, there's nearly always something to distract you from the hard work. Roots and rocks on technical climbs demand all your attention to conquer them, leaving you with no time to worry about how much your legs are howling. If you need proof that riding off-road is a lot less soul destroying than similar activities elsewhere, try riding up a big hill on the road with nothing but your ever diminishing speed and boiling legs for company. You'll be begging for a trail sign. Mountain biking gets you fit but it lets you have loads of fun while you're doing it. What other exercise offers you that?

A basic training guide

Before we get into the MTB specifics we need to explain the basics of why exercise makes you fitter, and how you can control that process to get the results you want.

Train properly and each ride will help you evolve further towards being the ultimate cyclist.

Personal evolution

Think 'evolution' and you probably have images of fish waddling onto land and monkeys standing up straight. But the same evolutionary forces are working inside us every day. Every time your body is exposed to stress it'll recover and strengthen itself to deal with that same stress again.

Every time your heart forces blood towards your muscles so that they can push down on the pedals to shove you up that hill, each part of the process is marked down for evolutionary improvement. The heart will increase slightly in size, with stronger muscles to squeeze it harder. The arteries will grow to pipe blood that's been modified to carry more fuel and oxygen. At the muscles more fibres will wait to take the fuel, process it faster then discard it more efficiently with a bit less pain and suffering. Even the nerves that control the motion will fire that bit faster and more smoothly next time. In short, if you're training properly each ride helps you evolve further towards being the ultimate cyclist.

Room to grow

All this growth requires room, fuel and time, which is why good rest is as crucial to fitness development as the workout itself. Muscles ache after a ride because their fibres are ragged and torn from exertion, and waste products from their last workout are still waiting to be flushed through with fresh blood. Work too hard now and a body empty of energy will just weep and fall over. Strained muscles will complain, blood too full of waste acids will be unable to fight viruses and you'll collapse in a feverish, limping, fainting mess. It's hard to improve your fitness in a day but it's easy to destroy your health with one hard session too many.

However, at the opposite end of the scale, if you leave your body for too long between its stress-stimulating sessions it'll save its energy for other 'improvements' (like laying down fat in case of a hard winter) and you won't improve at all.

Setting your sights

So how do you stay on the right side of the training gain curve without straying into the dangers of overtraining or just not improving at all? The key to this is establishing a gradually increasing series of goals and improvements that give you short term marker posts on the road to optimum fitness. The most important aspect of any fitness plan and the goal that it takes you towards is that it has to be achievable.

Don't plan on five sessions a week if you are only doing one and don't pencil in your Olympic medal in a couple of years if you've only ridden round the block once before. Match your immediate targets to what you can achieve now. If you can do your local loop in an hour and ten minutes now, aim to finish it in an hour and five minutes next month and under an hour within two months. That way you can hit achievable goals and tick them off as you progress.

Don't be too inflexible though. It may be that weather makes that local loop much slower, or perhaps you catch a cold that knocks you off your schedule for two weeks. Don't try and hit those same goals. Reset them to accommodate the changes.

For the best results, and so you don't just go cross-eyed with boredom, break that hour loop (or whatever your target is) down into component pieces. Work out where it is that you really slow down and where you gallop along. If you can hold cruising speed really well but grovel on the steep hill half way round, then train to solve the problem. Go to the hill (or find a nearer more convenient one) and practise riding that several times each session. You'll soon find yourself flying up the 'problem' hill on your loop, especially if you know you only have to do it once.

Whether you want to just ride up that hill without walking or want to wear the World Championship jersey on your shoulders, the way to go about it is exactly the same. Step by step, little by little. It really is how even the greatest champions start.

A favourite 'warm up' tool of pro riders, connecting a bike up to a stationary turbo trainer can be a good way to supplement your fitness programme.

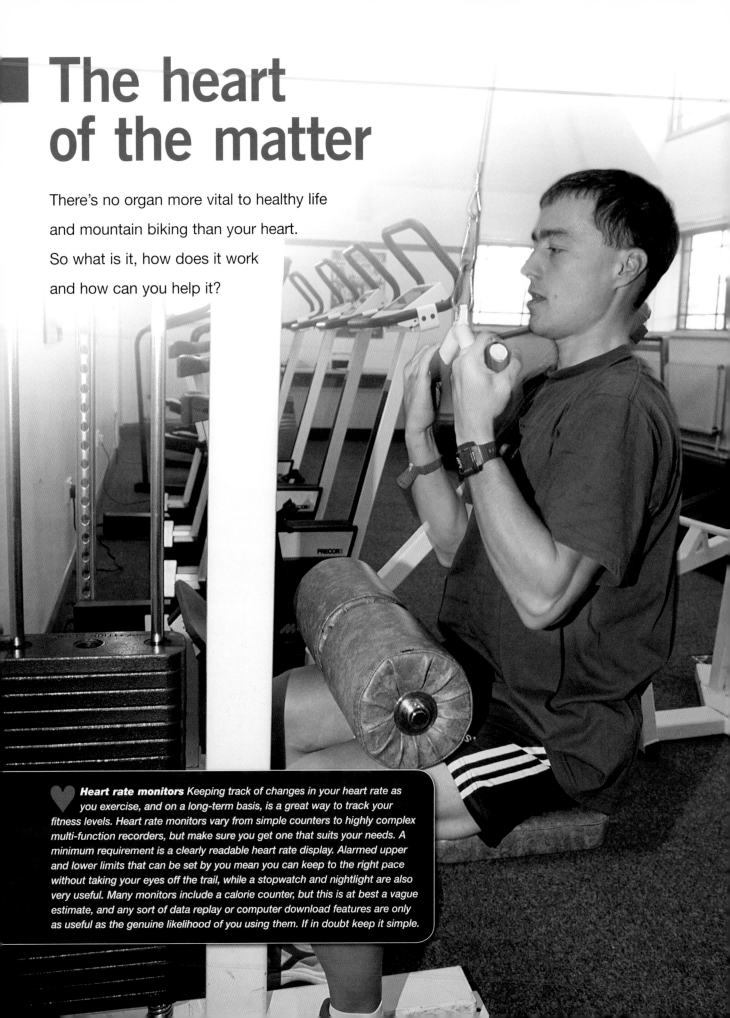

The heart of the matter

There's no organ more vital to healthy life and mountain biking than your heart. So what is it, how does it work and how can you help it?

Heart rate monitors *Keeping track of changes in your heart rate as you exercise, and on a long-term basis, is a great way to track your fitness levels. Heart rate monitors vary from simple counters to highly complex multi-function recorders, but make sure you get one that suits your needs. A minimum requirement is a clearly readable heart rate display. Alarmed upper and lower limits that can be set by you mean you can keep to the right pace without taking your eyes off the trail, while a stopwatch and nightlight are also very useful. Many monitors include a calorie counter, but this is at best a vague estimate, and any sort of data replay or computer download features are only as useful as the genuine likelihood of you using them. If in doubt keep it simple.*

What is your heart?

Forget all the love songs. Your heart is nothing more than a big muscular circulatory pump. With each muscle squeeze, blood comes into the right-hand side and then squirts out to the lungs. In the same 'beat' freshly oxygenated blood is sucked back into the left-hand side and pumped out to muscles, brain, vital organs and every other part of your body. The average human heart weighs about half a pound, and various examples have recorded between 12 and 240bpm (beats per minute), depending on fitness and genetic build. The average ticker does 70 to 80bmp at rest, pumping 36,000 litres of blood through 20,000km of blood vessels each and every day.

Some hearts are born larger than others, some are born beating faster, but either way your body will compensate, so don't worry what comes factory fitted. If you can exercise enough to raise your heart rate two or three times a week then you will be significantly increasing your health, in several ways. Your heart will become larger, fitter and stronger, helping it to cope better with stress. Your plumbing will become larger and faster flowing, and your internal organs will be able to call on increased blood flow whenever they need it.

Your circulation a guided tour

Just as important as the heart is the network of thousands of kilometres (yes, km) of tubing that carries blood all round your body and then brings it back again. Blood heading out from the heart travels through arteries, whose size depends on expected rate of flow, from huge pipes like the aorta to tiny, thin capillaries.

First stop is the lungs, where the blood is fanned out to individual air sacs, releasing carbon dioxide and taking in oxygen. It then goes back into the heart to pick up speed and head off round the body. Some blood heads upwards to the upper limbs and brain, dropping off oxygen, food and medical supplies and coming back with carbon dioxide and other waste products. Other blood pumps through the lower part of the body and legs, while the portal circulation loop gurgles past the stomach and intestines, before washing all that nutritional goodness it's collected into the liver for storage.

'Used' blood then heads back through the filter of the kidney towards the heart through the veins. The veins are also elastic tubes but they are fitted with small valves that stop back flow of blood. They're easily spotted on the surface by the blue colour of the oxygen-depleted blood inside them.

Training your heart

Like any muscle, the heart responds to regular hard work by getting big and strong. The bigger and stronger it gets, the more oxygen and fuel it can feed to the muscles, so the faster you can go. Heart rate measuring works as a guide to your exertion. The harder you ride your bike, the more oxygen and energy your muscles demand, so the faster the heart pumps to get it there. When you exert yourself it's not uncommon for the heart to beat five times faster than it does at rest.

Heart rate is now regularly used as an indicator of exercise effort, and a whole training and coaching culture has sprung up around heart rate 'zones', discussed in more detail later in this chapter. Before you start a serious exercise programme get a health check from your doctor who will advise suitable exercise levels for your current state of health.

Powerful heart equals powerful riding.

Converting air to speed

Breathing is the most essential bodily function – even your heart is no use unless it has oxygen to pump round. If you can't breathe, the vital systems of your body will fail and die within minutes in all but a few exceptional circumstances. As a mountain biker you'll know how hard you have to breathe to haul yourself up climbs and just how miserable life gets if you ride harder than your breathing can keep up. But what is involved in respiration? What happens between air going in and power coming out? What can you do to make the most of the partnership between your lungs and legs?

__Training aids__ There are two things that will help you to train accurately and exactly, significantly increasing the gain from each session. The first is a heart rate monitor, ideally with programmable high and low heart rate zones. Hi/Low alarms, a stopwatch and a light for night sessions are handy but a basic pulse readout is the only essential. The second major training aid is a stationary trainer that lets you spin your wheels indoors, ideal for when weather, traffic or trail conditions interrupt your training. Be warned though that using them will often be tougher on your boredom threshold than it is on your legs. Finally, for the truly serious athlete, there's training at altitude, or even sleeping in an altitude tent. Riding at 10,000 feet/3,300m or higher is where oxygen levels are thinner and the body has to overcompensate to suck in more. The effect gives you a sizeable, albeit short-lived, supercharged advantage when you return to lower altitudes.

Taking a breath

Your lungs are two big bags which hang inside your ribcage, above the diaphragm that separates your chest cavity from the rest of your guts. Air is sucked in when your chest muscles expand your ribcage and drop your diaphragm to create a vacuum that the lungs have to fill by pulling air in from the outside.

The average human Hoover will suck in a breath every four seconds, or 16 times a minute, but this will drop as the body becomes more efficient at extracting oxygen and using it around the body. When the body is resting, your lungs move about 0.5 litres of 'tidal' air in and out, but at full gasping power the average pair of lungs can move 3.5–4 litres of air. However hard you breathe out, a litre of 'residual' air will remain in your airways just to stop them sticking together.

The oxygen is absorbed by the haemoglobin cells in the blood (turning them red in the process) and then pumped round to the muscles by the heart. The muscles take the oxygen from the blood and replace it with the waste product carbon dioxide (turning the blood blue). The blood then flows back through the heart to the lungs to dump the carbon dioxide and pick up more oxygen.

Essential O_2

Oxygen is vital for the operation, division, repair of cells and internal organs right from your brain to your brawn. If your brain is starved of oxygen for only a few seconds, severe and permanent damage can occur.

Breathing is particularly important for endurance sports like mountain biking because of the way muscles obtain their energy during prolonged exercise. In simple terms, muscles derive energy from splitting sugary molecules stored in the body. If this reaction happens with enough O_2 present – 'aerobically' – then the sugary fuel is efficiently broken down into energy, water and carbon dioxide.

However, if you're demanding energy so fast – sprinting, etc – that your body can't supply enough oxygen, the reaction becomes anaerobic ('without oxygen'). Although it's fast, this process is hugely inefficient and wasteful of energy. The reaction also produces lactic acid, which is what causes that burning sensation in your muscles when you're flat out. For this reason, the more oxygen you can supply to the muscles, the faster and further you can ride efficiently without pain.

Turbocharging

Lung size is genetically pre-determined, as is the level of lactic acid your muscles produce when you work anaerobically. The good news is that with the right sort of training you can improve on the function of whatever body you were born with.

Training relies on providing enough regular stress to make your body adapt to cope. In this case we're working on creating a more efficient oxygen/waste product exchange system at both the lung and muscle ends of the breathing loop. Increased cardiac and respiratory fitness is gained from 50 per cent effort upwards, but gains are at their most rapid nearer the aerobic limit – typically 70 per cent of maximum effort. These 'threshold sessions' increase the body's ability to create energy efficiently rather than slipping into the fast-burn anaerobic zone. For more training information including trial sessions and details of the 'Zone' system, read on.

Wake up and smell the oxygen.

Muscle power

How do cycling specific muscles differ from normal muscles, and how can we look after them and make them work better? While mountain biking is an excellent all round exercise, there's no doubting that your leg muscles are responsible for most of the work.

What are muscles?

Muscles are composed of bundles of contracting fibres that respond to electrical signals from the nerves and brain. As muscles can only pull, not push, each muscle is balanced by other muscles that work in the other direction. The more work a muscle does, the larger it is. Muscles are often layered on top of each other, all working in slightly different directions doing different jobs.

How your muscles work on the bike

Every body movement is caused by groups of muscles working together. To press a pedal down, the buttock quadriceps (front of thigh) muscles contract to straighten the leg. The calf also contracts to transfer this force along the foot into the pedal. These muscles then relax as the pedal reaches the bottom of the stroke. The hamstrings (back of the thigh) then contract to bend the leg and pull it back up to the top of the pedal stroke where the whole process begins again. Throughout the pedal stroke, the muscles of the back and shoulders are also working to stabilise your hips, so it's the pedals that move, not you.

As a mountain biker contracts and releases these muscles thousands of times within a short ride, the muscles develop for maximum efficiency and stamina. This is why most regularly active riders tend to stay slim rather than building up bulging short-busting muscle.

Just like a well-oiled bike, your muscles work better if they are well maintained. Here's how…

Muscle training and technique

While your legs might seem to go round and round on the pedals fairly automatically, specific muscles are continually training and tidying up your technique. Your speed increases quickly for little extra effort.

Smoothness

Cycling is a rotary motion, which means the smoother and 'rounder' your stroke, the more efficiently you're using your muscles. As BMXers say, 'You gotta spin it to win it'.

Many road riders use 'fixed gear' bikes with no freewheel to encourage a smooth spin, but this would be lunacy off-road. Concentrate instead on spinning the pedals faster, and in a smooth circle rather than an up and down stomp. If you want to accelerate try to increase the speed of your legs rather than just changing up a gear. It takes a while to adjust and won't work in all technical trail situations but it's more efficient and less stressful on joints and muscles than heaving a big gear round.

Strength

There are times (such as deep mud or sudden steep climbs) when you'll need to deliver maximum power in a few pedal turns. To prepare your legs for this, practise using bigger than normal gears on climbs every now and again. Try this both in seated and standing positions as each uses slightly different combinations of muscles. Don't stomp, make your power delivery smooth and circular throughout the stroke, and next time it gets slippery you'll have far more traction than you expected.

Speed + Acid

The major limiting factor in speed is the point at which your body stops converting energy efficiently through using oxygen, and instead begins to 'suffocate', flooding your muscles with painful lactic acid. We cover this in more detail later, but by 'surfing' this line when you're training you'll increase oxygen delivery, heart volume and strength, muscular efficiency and your ability to tolerate and dispose of lactic acid.

Repeatedly taking your body to this limit, then resting, then hitting the limit again is known as interval training. As it conditions your body to flush away lactic acid quickly, you can make top speed gains very fast.

Muscle maintenance

Just like a well-oiled bike, your muscles work better if they are well maintained. Muscle fibres work much more smoothly and efficiently if they're supple and move easily past each other. Unfortunately, repeating the same exercise cycle thousands of times – exactly what you do when pedalling – actually shortens and stiffens the muscles. Straining muscles enough to develop them also causes microscopic 'fraying' and swelling of the fibres themselves, which together with lactic acid residue from anaerobic exercise causes stiffness and aching.

Physically stretching your muscles or moving them manually through massage restores the range of movement and stops fibres from sticking to one another. Think of it like brushing knots out of hair. So, like keeping dreadlocks at bay, it's best done regularly and frequently.

Cyclist's back

Lots of cyclists get bad backs. What should we do to prevent injuries, and why is back strength so important anyway? Aching legs might seem the obvious problem for mountain bikers, but bad backs are responsible for more people suffering on their bike in the long term or hanging up their helmet for good. Stomping legs, forward leaning position and the occasional crash combine with the continuous rattle and bump of mountain biking to put the body under loads it just wasn't designed for. A bad back won't just make it hard for you to ride, it'll make your whole life a chore.

How your bike fits you is vital to back comfort, so follow these tips to set it up right.

Bikers' backs

Your back is a big stack of vertebral bones divided by spinal cartilage discs which provide 'suspension' and allow the back to flex. Apart from crashes, skeletal damage is rare from mountain biking. Problems come from the muscles. The spinae erector runs from the pelvis to the base of the skull. This ensures that any stiffness in the legs, whose muscles attach to the lower stomach and buttock areas, automatically causes stiffness in the back. Limiting the movement of the back by keeping it in the same position for long periods of time (at work or on the bike) also tightens up muscles and increases the chance of injury.

Bike set up

How your bike fits you is vital to back comfort. The further forward you lean on the bike, the further you take your body from its normal upright position, causing muscles rather than spinal discs to absorb the shocks. However, too short a position can make it harder to breathe or to pull on the bars for acceleration, meaning more general tiredness on longer rides. Experiment with moving the saddle backwards or forwards and check frame stretch if you're buying a new one.

Saddle

Setting the saddle too high means the pelvis has to rock from side to side to reach the bottom of the pedal stroke. The back has to try and control this roll, which causes masses of strain and a rapid build up of tension. Check saddle height by sitting barefoot on the bike, spinning the cranks with your heels on the pedals. Your leg should be straight at the bottom of the pedal stroke – any wobble or stretch means your seat is too high.

Cockpit

Raising the handlebars creates a more upright riding position for less back strain. Fitting riser bars instead of flat bars adds height as well as extra width. Increasing bar width opens up the chest and shoulders as well as making steering lighter and easier to control. This all helps to reduce upper body tension, especially in very tight, technical riding situations. However, too wide a bar can stretch your shoulders too far, increasing fatigue, so don't go much beyond actual shoulder width.

Suspension

There's no doubt that suspension has made mountain biking a lot more comfortable, but this doesn't have to mean big springs and saggy forks. Suspension seat posts have soothed countless bikers' bad backs, while even bigger tyres or lower pressures can be enough to take the edge off the sharp shocks.

Gears

Even gear choice can have a big effect on comfort. Spinning a small gear in smooth circles means much less heaving, twisting and straining for the back, hips and shoulders and knees than stamping big gears around. Learning correct, smooth technique for wheelies, bunny hops, etc, will also save your body a lot of jarring compared to heaving on the bars and hoping for the best.

Daytime damage

Unfortunately most of us have to spend far more time working than we do riding, and this can damage the body as well as the mind. All office workers should make sure that they sit upright with bum pushed firmly into the back corner of the chair. Don't lean forwards and keep your shoulders relaxed and open rather than hunched forward. Make an excuse to get up every hour for a circulation restoring stroll and, if you spend a lot of time on the phone, ask for a hands-free headset. Manual workers are more active, but try to avoid repeating the same movement over and over again in exactly the same way. Remember to bend those knees and ask for a hand when picking up heavy objects. Finally, couch slouch is a business boost for chiropractors – think carefully about your posture as you watch TV, and why not do a few stretches while you're at it.

An ideal bike set-up and ride posture gives you the best potential for powerful riding, especially on climbs.

Food

How does food create energy and what should mountain bikers be eating? For many riders deciding what to eat is a case of finishing their ride and grabbing the nearest vaguely edible substance first, then devouring anything else in sight until they stop feeling hungry. However, not all foods are created equal and getting your fuel mixture right or wrong can make a huge difference to your riding and enjoyment.

Turning food into energy

The body can only store a few seconds worth of energy in the muscles but can quickly replace it by breaking down food-based fuel. The various food constituents are released through digestion and then stored around the body until you need them.

Carbohydrates contain 4kcal per gram but are the easiest fuel to access as they are stored in the muscles and liver as 'glycogen'. Protein also contains 4kcal per gram but these are mainly used to build and repair muscles and organs. They will only be broken down to provide fuel if other glycogen reserves are exhausted.

Fat contains the most energy per gram at 9kcal, but takes longer for the body to break down during digestion, and is slower to be converted into energy. Your body will use mostly fat derived energy when riding slowly, but will burn carbohydrates when you work harder. Vitamins and minerals are also vital for allowing and helping chemical reactions for building, repair or energy purposes within the body.

When to eat

Don't have a big meal straight before a ride. Top up with a carbohydrate snack (couple of bananas, jam sandwich, energy bar, etc) shortly before exercise. On rides of over an hour, use a carbohydrate drink or snack to offset energy loss and have another snack straight after exercise as your body will refill your energy reserves double quick. Always take an extra 'emergency' energy bar or snack too. If you suddenly start to feel what cyclists will often refer to as 'hunger knock' or 'bonk' (basically feeling faint from low blood sugar) wolf your snack down pronto with plenty of water, and ease off the pace until you feel recovered.

Know your nosh

Luckily, food is one of those rare products that has to declare exactly what it contains before you buy it, so you can control the fat, protein and carbohydrate levels you eat. To keep yourself refuelled and ready to ride, carbohydrates should form 60–70 per cent of your total calories. To keep your body repairing and building smoothly, 15–20 per cent of your total calories should come from protein. The rest of your food can be fat, but remember that fat contains over double the calories of protein and carbohydrate so a little goes a long way toward your total calories intake.

Vitamins and minerals should be obtained from that classic dose of 'five fruit or vegetables per day'. You'll also need enough water to keep all this mixture swilling through, so drink regularly and always have a glass with your meal.

The right stuff

There's a whole load of food occupying supermarket shelves, trying to tempt us with claims of healthiness or suitability for an 'active lifestyle', but what should you actually eat? Rice, potatoes and bread are the fastest absorbed of the carbohydrates, with the added advantage that at least one of them can be included in most meals. Breakfast cereals and muesli are an excellent high energy snack for any time of the day. Noodles and pasta take a little longer to digest, as do porridge and bran cereals, but they all provide top quality medium-term energy. Beans and pulses are fairly low in carbohydrates, but they give a useful slow burn source for an otherwise fast absorbed meal.

However you get your carbohydrate just make sure you boil, grill or steam it rather than frying it in fat.

The difficulty with getting protein into your diet is that it often goes hand in hand with fat. Tuna or lean meat are top sources for carnivores, but veggies will have to chow down a large amount of soya, skimmed milk and beans to keep up.

Fat is an essential part of the diet but only in moderation. Plump for the healthier fats in olive oil, oily fish and nuts, rather than loading yourself with saturated lard.

Food on the go

It may be easy to keep things balanced when you're in the kitchen, but what food should be coming riding with you? Energy bars are theoretically the perfect balanced solid fuel, but they need swilling through with a lot of water or they will just sit in your stomach. Fig rolls, bananas or other dried fruit generally work as well for a lot less money.

Powders, drinks and gels are based on modified starch maltodextrins and polymers. These have the advantage of being faster absorbed, but you'll still need to swill them through with plenty of water unless they're low concentration.

Weight loss

Mountain biking is strenuous but enjoyable. It's an excellent weight loss exercise, but dieting while biking needs to be done carefully and slowly. Never aim to reduce your weight by more than 2lb a week, and never cut more than 500kcal from your daily calorie intake in a two-week period. Extreme low calorie or low carbohydrate diets cause muscle wasting rather than fat loss, while exhaustion and dizziness will make riding extremely dangerous.

Instead of conventional dieting, it's best to combine a small drop in fat and overall calorie consumption with a small increase in time spent on the bike. For example, drop 250kcal from your diet and ride steadily for an extra half hour and you'll still be saving 500kcal per day. Don't ride when starved though as you'll burn muscle not fat – it's better to snack before and eat less later.

Always pack a mid-ride snack to keep your energy up. A Power Bar or fruit such as bananas are ideal.

Avoid big meals right before a ride and try and opt for healthier fats – which means cutting back on the fry-ups!

Drink

Water is as crucial as food to mountain bikers. But why, how much do we need, and what are the best ways of carrying it? We're not saying you're wet, but water makes up 90 per cent of a human body. Leave a human in the sun for long enough and all that's left is a large rawhide dog chew with a selection of bones inside. Even if you start losing a few per cent of that water you're risking serious problems for keeping body and soul together. Most of us have a drinking problem we never even knew about.

Drinking little and often is the best way to replace the fluids you lose through sweating and exertion.

Hydrate or die! *The thicker blood gets, the harder it is for the heart to pump it and the less volume there is to do the work. Also, the more you dehydrate the less your body can sweat, so the faster the heat builds up. This means your body has to work harder and hotter and the problem spirals out of control very quickly. Water loss equal to 2 per cent of bodyweight equates to a performance loss of 10–20 per cent. Four per cent dehydration can cause vomiting, nausea and diarrhoea as the body evacuates food it can't process. Five per cent dehydration equates to a performance loss of 10–30 per cent. Eight per cent dehydration can trigger weakness, dizziness, confusion and laboured breathing, while losses beyond that will often result in hospitalisation and possible long-term damage.*

There are two main ways to carry fluids on your bike; with a water bottle fitted to your frame or a hydration pack (left).

So why do you need all this water?

Our bodies use water for all manner of different functions. Sweating regulates our body temperature by increasing the heat conductivity of the skin and evaporating heat away in sweaty vapour. Water also forms the basis for all the fluids and lubricants that keep our bodies working. Blood plasma, synovial fluid around joints, cell regeneration, muscles, nerves, brain, bones, skin, lungs, etc, are all totally dependent on water-based fluids for operation. There's a direct link between water and food as well, as food can't be digested without it.

Drink up

On average the human body loses between 0.75 and 1 litre of fluid per hour of exercise. This could increase to over 2 litres per hour for hard work in hot and/or humid conditions. Always err on the side of caution and try to drink at least 2 litres of water a day on top of your exercise requirements.

The best way to check if you're drinking enough is to check the colour of your urine. If you're fully hydrated, your urine will be completely clear. The more dehydrated you are, the more concentrated the urea (waste products) will be and the more yellowy your urine will appear.

Beyond water

Water is an excellent thirst quencher for short rides but there's a big choice of other drinks out there. Fluid replacement drinks can be absorbed by the body faster than pure water. They do this by including a smaller amount (4 per cent) of minerals or carbohydrate/sugars than the body's own fluids, so absorption is rapid and no extra fluid is taken from the gut. They are excellent for use in prolonged high sweat loss situations.

Isotonic drinks are absorbed by the body as fast as pure water but they also carry significant fuel (4–8 per cent) for the muscles. These drinks are an excellent choice for long rides where you need to replace fluid and fuel. Concentrated (8 per cent-plus) energy drinks need additional water from the body before they can be absorbed.

Energy 'Gels' are the ultimate sticky energy concentrate for pure energy intake with minimum bulk but they need a lot of water with them to allow the body to break them down efficiently.

Recovery drinks contain carbohydrates, electrolytes and vitamins to replace those lost when you're exercising, as well as protein to quicken their absorption.

When is a drink not a drink?

Just because it's wet doesn't mean it will properly quench your thirst. Drinks with too much sugar (soft drinks, fruit juices and concentrated energy drinks) need more water to process them than they contain. Alcohol and caffeine drinks are also best avoided as they make you pee.

Inflight refuelling

There are two main ways to carry water on your bike. Traditional water bottles are cheap and disposable, but not all bikes can carry them, they are harder to reach on the move and they can get covered in muck. Hydration packs, such as Camelbaks, and other rucksacks that contain a water bladder, can be used hands-free. They stay cleaner and can carry a lot more water. Not everyone likes the weight on their back though and they are more expensive.

Fluid replacement drinks are widely available and are ideal for longer rides as they can be absorbed by the body faster than pure H_2O.

Fitness tailoring

How and when should you train for specific aims? Riding your mountain bike will see you gain fitness almost by accident, but if you want to get fitter as fast as possible then you need to do some specific training. The most commonly accepted basis for fitness programmes are the five training 'zones'. These correspond to different levels of exertion, and the effects that training at these intensities have on your body.

Zone warrior The five zones are normally worked out as follows:

Level/Zone 1: Healthy heart zone. 50–60% of HRR. This level lowers blood pressure and gently exercises the heart. It also works as active recovery for trained athletes.

Level/Zone 2: Temperate zone. 60–70% of HRR. This level increases heart fitness and the body burns a high proportion of fat.

Level/Zone 3: Aerobic zone. 70–80% of HRR. This level increases the heart, muscle and lung efficiency for long-range stamina.

Level/Zone 4: Threshold zone. 80–90% of HRR. This is the boundary level between efficient sustained aerobic work with enough oxygen and less efficient fast burn anaerobic work where not enough oxygen is present. You'll feel the boundary change as a 'burning' sensation as your oxygen starved muscles start to produce lactic acid.

Level/Zone 5: Redline zone. 90–100% of HRR. This level is essentially flat out, short burst exertion. Only recommended for trained athletes.

All of these figures are general guidelines but don't be surprised if you've previously been working much harder than you thought.

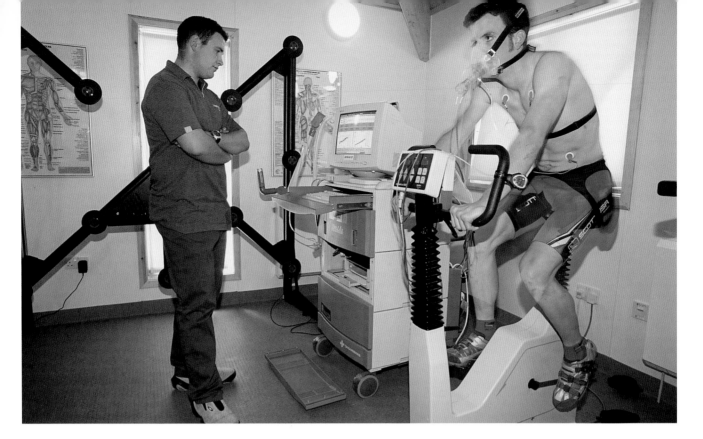

Get set, go

If you're new to this exercise lark, even if you think you used to be fit, get yourself an MoT from your doctor before going flat out. Even if you exercise regularly don't try to suddenly increase your workload. You may feel great for a couple of weeks then keel over. As a rule, never increase your training workload (in time or intensity) by more than 10 per cent in a week.

Once you've got the all clear you need to establish your maximum heart rate. There are all sorts of 'lab testing' ways of doing this but you'll get a pretty accurate idea by checking what your monitor reads when you're riding as hard as you can. This will usually mean warming up for a good 20 minutes or so then sprinting uphill.

The next parameter is your resting heart rate. Again just check your heart rate regularly when you're rested. Sitting still reading before bed or just after waking up is the best time. You'll find the average reading after a week or so. Subtract this figure from your maximum heart rate and you have your 'heart rate reserve' (HRR). You'll be able to work out your zone percentages from your HRR and then add your resting heart rate to give the actual bpm zone limits. Read on for more info on this.

How often?

It's all too easy to exhaust your body faster than your enthusiasm. If you start training specifically you will probably exert yourself more in a given time than on a general ride, so don't be tempted to increase the frequency of your cycling until you know you can cope. A good guideline is to increase your training effort by no more than 10 per cent per week either in time or intensity. Keep a check of resting heart rate to make sure you're not overdoing things.

On the programme

To work out a simple programme train in the zones that give the results you're after. Remember that the higher up the zones you go or the longer you stay in them, the more time it takes to recover, so keep an eye on that resting heart rate.

Keep your training varied by fitting in sessions from zones either side of your normal target zone too, otherwise you'll develop too specific a fitness, which will be little use on varied intensity MTB rides.

Warming up and warming down

It is crucial that you give your heart and blood vessels time to prepare themselves properly before pushing too hard. As a guide aim to increase intensity gradually for 10 minutes when warming up and then reverse the process after a hard ride.

When to stop

Resting heart rate is an excellent guide to your fatigue levels. If it's over 10 per cent higher than normal then your body hasn't fully recovered yet so take a rest the next day. If it's over 10 per cent lower than normal then your body is exhausted so take at least two days off. However don't be at all surprised if your heart rate gradually drops as you progress in your training programme. The bigger and stronger your heart becomes by training hard, the slower it needs to pump to maintain resting blood circulation.

Keep an eye on your resting heart rate to gauge your fatigue levels. There's plenty of hi-tech equipment out there to help you do this, but a finger on your pulse and a wristwatch does the job.

Race fitness

So you've got your head around the basic fitness theories. What about specific techniques for specific goals? Sprints, intervals, endurance and lactate tolerance training all play their part. Training zones form a good set of basic exercise building blocks, but for peak performance, a series of specific training sessions will make the best use of your time.

Endurance races demand maximum performance, stamina and fitness. You can achieve this by tweaking your training regime.

Work on your weaknesses

The first thing to do before you even start training is work out where you most need to improve. By working on your weaknesses you'll see much faster overall fitness gains than if you try and improve areas where you are already strong.

For example, if you can ride all day at the same speed but can't sprint to save your life you'll start to improve by getting in some flat-out 10 second sprint sessions. On the other hand, if you can beat every pizza moped in town away from the traffic lights but you flake out on rides over 10 miles then you need to put in some steady long-range rides to get your head and body used to cruising.

Make notes of your progress and personal best times and set yourself goals to keep motivation high. Make sure they're always realistically achievable though, that way you'll feel good about training rather than trying to hit unrealistically high targets too soon.

Once you've worked out which areas need work and set yourself some targets use our selection of training sessions to get you there.

Endurance training

Riding long distances at a steady pace uses a completely different set of fuel and fitness requirements to short sharp sprints. The best way to train your base aerobic fitness and the fatty fuel systems that power it is to do long Level 2–3 rides. Gradually make them longer and further as you get used to them but always take enough food and water with you to avoid tears, and try and rope in another rider or two for company.

Interval sessions

By revving you up and then resting you, interval sessions enable you to spend longer in a target zone than continuous threshold sessions. They also train your recovery mechanism, allowing rapid increases in aerobic fitness. Intervals can be anything from 10 seconds to an hour in length but the following selection are proven winners…

- **Cruise control** Warm up steadily for 10 minutes. Start stopwatch and accelerate to aerobic threshold level (Zone 4), and hold for five minutes. Relax and spin for a minute before accelerating up to threshold again. Start with five threshold stints a session and build up gradually to eight or ten stints. Always warm down gently afterwards.
- **Retch and recovery** This brutal session will increase your anaerobic lactic acid tolerance and your recovery rate in maximum power situations. Warm up steadily for ten minutes. Sprint flat-out uphill for 30 seconds. Freewheel back down for 30 seconds. Repeat two more times then rest for five minutes before doing the full set again. Increase by one sprint per set each subsequent session, until you reach five sprints per set. Then increase to three sets of three before building up to three sets of five.

Cross training

Whether it's the weather or mechanical misery that's getting in the way you can also make significant fitness gains without your bike.

- **Spinning** is a gym based stationary bike workout which takes boredom and loneliness out of indoor sessions.
- **Running** is a high intensity workout that pushes heart rates and oxygen uptake higher than any other exercise. Start gently to avoid impact injuries and always stretch rigorously afterwards.
- **Swimming** trains your body to work on whatever limited oxygen you can gasp from above the water and has no impact injury dangers.
- **Gym work** with weights can help anaerobic power and recovery, while rowing machines, treadmills, stair climbers and elliptical trainers will all work your cardio-respiratory system. Like running, your threshold levels will differ depending on each exercise.

Psychological training

For racers, the strength of your mind is every bit as important as the strength in your legs. The key to this is relaxed confidence and the way to this peace of mind is through rehearsing and visualising each likely situation in your head.

Before each training session or race work out what you want to do and rehearse how you're likely to feel at each part. See yourself working through the pain and not giving up on that last sprint. Reinforce positive thoughts or you'll just set yourself up to fail. Best of all, you can do this training from the comfort of your couch, so it's got to be worth a try hasn't it?

There are plenty of other activities you can do off the bike to work your heart rate. Try running, swimming and sex!

Biking benefits

While it may mean more dirty washing to cope with,
and the occasional bruise or scratch if you ride hard,
mountain biking can do wonders for your body and soul.

Body

We've seen how biking can turn even the most rooted couch potato into a mean, lean cardiovascular revelation, but how will his affect the rest of your life?

Energy

For a start, as a regular exerciser you'll have a lot more energy and find everything else you do a whole lot easier so you can do more of it, or use your new energy to do other exciting things. You'll also carry this new energy and vitality into a longer life as your new improved heart carries on ticking and you burn your fat off up the hills. Better than finding that your favourite armchair seems to get tighter by the day, until it's suddenly the heart in your chest, not your chair, that's seizing.

Ecstasy

Your body will also be buzzing with a whole new series of pleasures. The zip of adrenalin from close shaves or uphill charges, the warm fuzzy glow of endorphin in tired legs or just the giddy open mouthed grin that mountain biking so often delivers. Even the most boring office job is more bearable if you know you'll be careering through the local woods that evening, or those idle out of the window moments are spent planning the next big weekend ride.

Life

If you're a social type you have a whole new reason to go up and accost total strangers, and many lifelong friendships have been struck up after a casual query about reliability of a certain fork or the squeaking of a particular brake. You'll never be short of stupid stories or anecdotes to enliven conversation either, even if you were out riding when a current 'must watch' TV show is on.

Even romance can blossom by the trailside, and in these circumstances all that newly freed blood flow and increased stamina will open up a whole new cornucopia of delights when the high performance garments have been shed.

Lust

On those lonely evenings when even the cat has gone next door, your bike is a constant companion. It will never refuse a bit of polishing or gentle petting and may even repay your affection with a faultless ride next time out. Even if it doesn't always work so well after you've 'fixed it', that means a whole slew of exciting shopping opportunities. Glossy magazines full of tempting techno porn or the irresistible urges bought on by a well-lit down-town bike shop window. A serious mountain bike habit will cheerily swallow any amount of money and think nothing of demanding more a few days later.

Anger

Stress is a standard issue in most people's lives these days. Pressures of work, relationships, traffic and a host of other nightmares or niggles all constantly conspire to turn simmering discontent into a full-blown boiling rage at some point or other.

But why risk venting your spleen at entirely the wrong person when you already have the perfect anger management tool in your possession? Fit to strangle the boss or bludgeon your significant other into agreement over who did the washing up last? Grab your bike, head for the nearest hill and just let rip. All that anger and frustration will pour from your sweat glands and put the fire in your pedalling belly until that negativity is just a distant memory.

With all its demands on your attention, mountain biking is also an ideal way to wipe your mind-slate clean while you're riding. That approaching drop-off will have no trouble shoving any worries about an unpaid bill to the back of your mind, and when you're out in the middle of nowhere you've left that dimly lit office far behind both mentally and physically.

Calm

Sitting silently on a peak or in a favourite clearing of your local wood, mountain biking offers the ultimate in calming karma. There's no easier or faster way to leave civilisation behind in favour of trees, moors and rolling hills. Even the effort of getting there has its own soothing rhythm. Each little rise gained or log hopped is another diversion from stress, another barrier between you and your worries. Tired, contented and calm, but buzzing within, it's how all mountain bike rides should end.

Fun and games

But while we might wheel out all these perfectly tenable arguments as to why mountain biking is the path to enlightened happiness, the best thing about it is the fact it's good daft fun. You get filthy, muck about, take risks, crash, break things, race people, and chase people in a way you probably haven't since your primary school playground.

Mountain biking is a funny old world, but above all it's a fun one.

Mud splattered but smiling: blatting around on your MTB is fun.

Get out on your MTB to mess around with mates, beat stress, get fit and you'll be happier and healthier, guaranteed.

CHAPTER 5

Bike anatomy – chassis

Buying a mountain bike is not as easy as it used to be. As well as the traditional 'diamond' framed 'hardtail', which comes in several price and style categories, there is an ever-expanding range of full suspension bikes aimed at every rider type. And then you have to learn all about which construction materials are best, or at least which are best suited to your chosen ride style or price range. It's a can of worms, but this chapter can help you to unravel at least part of the puzzle.

Suspension forks are now commonplace and offer increased levels of control and comfort.

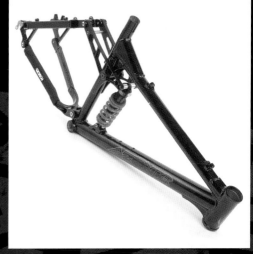

Rear suspension is chosen for more demanding and aggressive terrain.

The basic hardtail

The hardtail mountain bike is a direct descendant of the classic double diamond shaped bike. It's the easiest and most efficient way of joining the rider, the pedals and the wheels together. It's only the relatively recent rise of front and rear suspension that's seen the old motorbike term 'hardtail' being adopted to describe bikes with rigid frames.

Joining the dots

The classic hardtail is an outwardly straightforward structure, usually formed from eight tubes and a handful of special junction pieces, but it isn't that simple when you get close up.

So, why buy a hardtail?

They might bounce you around and make you ache more than suspension bikes, but there are still plenty of good reasons to buy a classic hardtail.

For a start the lack of springs and pivots means that they are lighter and simpler to look after than suspension bikes. As a result they accelerate faster and don't break down as often. This means you get to spend more time travelling fast. They're easier to attach things to or pick up than most suspension bikes. This makes them the perfect do-everything bike whether you're commuting on slick tyres, carrying kiddie seats, heading off transcontinental touring far from the nearest shock service centre or shopping with panniers and a trailer.

While hardtails might rattle around more-off road, many riders actually prefer them because of that. Reasons are many and varied, ranging from lack of squish or wallow on climbs to enjoying having to use your skills to steer careful lines at 10mph rather than suddenly finding yourself ploughing a carefree furrow over the top of everything at 20mph on a long travel full suspension bike. Ten miles per hour is a much friendlier speed to hit trees at, and it keeps local riding exciting rather than demanding big hills to play on. Finally, some people just find the whole aesthetics of extra linkages, pivots and shocks ugly compared to the simple style of a classic hardtail.

Dropouts hold the rear wheel in place. They often appear to receive as much cosmetic attention as all the rest put together. There are tiny cowled steel units, big latticed or looped aluminium showpieces, laser cut titanium sections, special models for through-axles, bottle opener add-ons – some even have the bike builder's logo and/or frame number etched in. In practical terms forward facing or vertical slotted dropout designs are the most common, while rearward horizontal dropouts give singlespeed options and possibly extra strength.

Seatstays might appear to be the forgotten pipe of the frame, but their shape and size is vital to how much ground shock is transmitted from the back wheel to the saddle. Big bends look trendy and allegedly help to stop V-type brakes flexing, but as a general rule it's the diameter that matters: big will be bottom-bruising (cue better padded saddle), while skinny will generally tone down the shocks. Two-into-one wishbone type designs, conventional A frame or even extended 'Triple Triangle' designs are more attention grabbing than ride altering.

Chainstays not only have to resist the crushing and twisting pedalling forces between the bottom bracket and the rear axle but they also have to snake around the fat tyres and the crankarms that get in the way. Cue all sorts of cunning tube shapes and designs from ovals and circles to squares, with kinked and dented sections or in some cases the whole lot in one multi-curved pipe. As if all that isn't enough, you might even be treated to bracing pipes or intricately shaped bridge pieces behind the bottom bracket.

The bottom bracket is a specially cast tube that sits sideways in the frame to carry the crank bearings. The down tube, chainstays and seat tube all attach here and the whole area has to survive a serious amount of stress. Thankfully they all come with standardised threads now, but they still appear in two widths (68mm or 73mm).

The seat tube carries the seat post and saddle and, like the head tube, its angle is critical to the handling of the bike. 73 degrees is the industry standard measurement with 74 degrees for really sharp and immediate steering or 72 degrees on more relaxed bikes. Different bikes also need different sized seat posts (26.8mm to 31.6mm).

The top tube, or crossbar as it's often known, joins the head tube to the seat tube to stop it waggling about, but otherwise is one of the least stressed tubes on the bike. The down tube is the backbone of the bike that joins the head tube to the bottom bracket, keeping the steering and pedalling centres locked in line and handling big front end impacts. This is why it is usually the largest and most obviously shaped frame pipe.

The head tube is the short pipe that the forks slide into. On most bikes it is angled to operate between 70.5 and 71.5 degrees to create the best balance of steering, although downhill bikes use a slacker (between 68 and 70 degrees) angle for more stable high speed steering. Also, frames with suspension forks may sometimes be slacker angled until you climb aboard and the suspension fork sags.

The suspension fork

Suspension forks have become a standard fitment on most MTBs. A good suspension fork undoubtedly adds enough control and comfort to offset its weight disadvantage. A poor suspension fork adds some comfort, but the weight gain and control advantages are borderline. Knowing what to look for when choosing a fork, as well as how to keep it working, is a vital prerequisite to getting the most from it.

Market leader Rock Shox makes forks to suit every demand, from big hit downhill to superlight cross country, as shown here with the always desirable SID.

Why use suspension forks?

They're heavier, they're more expensive and they need far more care and attention than rigid forks so why are suspension forks so common? By absorbing the bumps on the ground before they get to the rest of the bike, and your upper body, a suspension fork makes your ride much more comfortable. It also stops your bike being thrown about, giving you a lot more control.

A well-controlled suspension fork will also keep the front wheel following the ground contours better so you'll have more traction for corners and braking. Some riders moan that they're wasting energy by 'bobbing' up and down when climbing, but by absorbing the bumps that would otherwise slow the bike down or push it off line, a good fork will ensure that all but the smoothest climbs are ridden faster.

Which spring?

Air springs are much lighter than other spring types and air pressure can be easily tuned to suit rider weight and style. Tight air seals often mean that initial friction is high, and air springs will always 'ramp up' through their travel, but this suits many riders. Many top end forks use a negative spring to help compress the fork. This makes them plusher over small bumps.

The coil spring, usually made of steel, is usually the smoothest spring type. It offers a constant resistance through its travel and there's no real possibility of it failing, making it an excellent choice for hard-hitting riders. On the downside, springs need to be swapped to tune to different rider weights, and they're way heavier than air.

Elastomer springs are like bouncy lumps of rubber with different spring weights denoted by different colours. They're still common in cheaper forks as

they're relatively light and simple, but they're less plush than a coil spring and not as light as air. Different rubbers can be used to tune spring rate, but performance can change with hot or cold weather and they go saggy with age.

Maintenance

Some forks rely on grease to keep them sliding smoothly. An increasing number rely on oil swilling about inside. Whatever it uses, the fork will need stripping and cleaning regularly, basically to stop grime and grit from causing seizures and scratches. The dirtier the riding the more often you'll have to service your forks.

DT Swiss bought UK pioneering fork brand Pace a while back. They're now seen as the classiest, and are possibly the most expensive, forks on the market.

The full suspension frame

Bicycles were one of the last vehicles to switch to suspension, but now they've made up for lost time with a decade of rapid development. With such a wide range of full suspension bikes on the market, just what do you need to know to put a spring in your step?

Why a full suspension bike?

Like suspension forks, bikes with rear suspension are invariably a fair bit heavier and more costly than similarly equipped hardtails. This is, in the main, because of the extra frame hardware required to make the rear suspension work well. As with forks, some riders are initially put off by shock movement when pedalling. But the added control and traction of suspension bikes means they're definitely faster in most situations, even up steep bumpy climbs. This has made them more and more popular with everyone from top level racers to novice riders, and now even mid-range full suspension bikes offer impressive performance.

Despite these advantages, some riders prefer the simplicity, immediate feel and challenge of riding a hardtail rather than making things easier with full suspension. Don't expect the hardtail to disappear.

Maintenance

As most systems rely either on solid bushings or replaceable cartridge bearing pivots, maintenance is normally a case of running things until they fall apart. But you can increase their lifespan. Regular wiping of all frame areas around the linkages will stop grit from building up, and packing bushes with grease makes them run quieter and smoother than leaving them to dry as the manuals often recommend. Apart from that, try to avoid direct blasts from jetwashes or degreasing lubricants, and do check bolts, bearings and bushings regularly for looseness.

Some ideas you need to know about

There are many full suspension designs (too many to mention here) that skirt around the main categories. Most are focused on the following, but some combine ideas from several systems…

Specialized four bar linkage designs seem to look a little different every year but they're still the undisputed market leader for bikes of this type.

The four bar linkage. This system, simply put, uses four 'bars' to form a rectangle within the frame structure, with each bar pivoting on the next one. The four bars are usually the chainstay, the seatstay, an added 'linkage' section and part of the frame itself. Four bar linkage systems allow a change of the rear wheel axle path and positioning of the shock wherever you want. A shock can also be isolated from sideways suspension loadings.

Linkages also allow almost whatever travel and leverage combinations the bike designer deems useful. The disadvantages are that the extra linkages or frame parts mean extra weight and extra bearings generally mean extra maintenance and more alignment difficulties.

Virtual Pivot Points: By using 'floating' linkages on rockers between the mainframe and rear subframe (or swingarm) the rear axle can be made to track around a Virtual Pivot Point (VPP). The idea is to isolate the rear axle from the pedal forces to give a smooth suspension action and bob free traction, although weight shifts still cause the suspension to bob if you don't have some sort of 'platform damped' shock fitted.

Platform Damping: Shock damping is a method of preventing a spring from bouncing uncontrollably. Platform damping is a way of dialling out weight shift and pedal force activated bob without overly compromising the shock's ability to react to bumps. Most platform damped shocks will allow you to choose a 'break point' at which you want the suspension to start dealing with bumps.

Soft-tail: A soft-tail is essentially a hardtail that allows vertical flex in the chainstays and has a shock mounted between the upper seatstays and the frame. Although it only gives an inch or so of travel, it is low weight, simple and helps to smooth edges off sharp hits for long ride comfort.

Horst Link: The licence for this well-regarded four-bar linkage system is owned by Specialized. The 'FSR' linkage uses a pivot on the chainstay ahead of the rear wheel. This allows the wheel to track with a modified axle path rather than the simple swingarm arc that comes with 'faux bar' linkage set-ups with the dropout pivot on the seat stays.

Specialized Brain: This 'FSR' four-bar linkage design uses a specially-developed two-part shock with an inertia valve positioned near the rear axle. The shock senses movement from the ground but stays stable as you're pedalling over smooth terrain.

Maverick Monolink: The Monolink system uses a linkage that includes the bottom bracket to span the front and rear sub-frames. This gives an upward and rearward axle path free from pedal feedback. The shock is a structural part of the rear triangle. It's been licensed by Klein for the Palamino, as well as Seven and Sycip.

DW Link: Dave Weagle (DW) registered this design, and several frame-makers use it. Theoretically, whatever gear you're in, squat and pedal feedback is counter-balanced without affecting the bump sensitivity. At its best, this equates to smooth small bump responses for great traction, a predictable and easy to control ride feel on terrain that's hard to read, plus a stable pedalling platform on uphill sections.

Rocker Linkage: This includes any system using a linkage that pivots around it's mid-point. The shock's at one end and the rest of the suspension system is at the other. It allows designers to tune shock leverage and position, and can be useful on many different systems.

GT i Drive: An idiosyncratic but effective system using a 'dog bone' linkage driving an eccentrically revolving bottom bracket mounting to isolate pedal feedback. The drive train effectively hangs underneath the bike, link-connected to both the swingarm and the main frame.

There are loads of different ways you can design a swingarm-based suspension bike, starting with simple wheel axle curves and culminating with virtual pivot systems with compression and axle paths that change depending on which gear you're in or how hard you're pedalling. There is no one 'best' way to do it.

The rear shock

As full suspension has developed, rear shocks have become much more advanced and more important to how your bike rides. So how do they work and how can you tune them? There are two basic types of shock you will come across – air and coil. Air shocks use compressed air as a spring. They are light in weight and easily adjustable, using a shock pump. They always offer a 'rising' or 'progressive' rate, which means they get increasingly stiff towards the end of the compression stroke.

Setting up *Shock adjustment makes little difference unless you get it just right. Different systems and riding styles require slightly different settings. The following basics are a good starting point...*

How soft? *Your suspension should 'sag' between 20 and 30 per cent of its full travel when you sit on the bike. Use a zip tie or grease on the shock as a guide. Sag allows suspension to extend into depressions as well as to compress. This gives maximum cornering and power traction. If there's not enough sag, reduce the air pressure or fit softer springs. If there's too much sag, get harder springs or add air pressure.*

How much damping? *Compression should be set as fast as possible for a plush feel, but not so fast it allows excessive bottoming out (getting to the end of its travel). Rebound should be set fast enough for a quick return during successive hits, or for rough ground traction, but not so fast that the rear end leaps up from the ground after compression. As a rule of thumb the suspension should work 'one and a half times' after a big hit. Imagine full compression to full extension then settling back to the normal level of sag.*

Coil shocks use a steel (or sometimes titanium) spring wrapped around a piston containing the damping fluid. They are heavier than air shocks but typically feel smoother and the coil spring means you can still ride (bouncily) home even if the damping fails. Different rider weights will demand different spring strengths, and springs can also be bought with constant or increasing rates of resistance to suit different bikes.

Some coil shocks also use a supplementary air spring to increase the load needed to compress them initially. Conversely, some air shocks use a small coil spring to help soften initial compression. Others use air chambers to increase the force needed at the end of the compression stroke to create a rising rate.

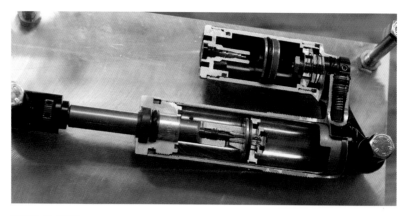

Damping

As with forks, rear shocks need damping systems to slow down spring compression and rebound, and help absorb bump forces. A piston moving through oil is the normal answer. Variable piston apertures will allow adjustment of the damping speed to suit the bike and spring used. Basic shocks will probably have factory set (non adjustable) compression and rebound damping.

Rebound damping is the most common simple external adjustment, and adjustable compression damping makes an appearance on better shocks. 'Lockout' levers are becoming increasingly common – they effectively 'switch off' the suspension, turning the bike into a hardtail for smooth climbs or road sections.

More advanced shocks have 'position sensitive' damping that changes as the shock compresses, helping to prevent it reaching full travel with a thump. Others might have separate damping systems for 'slow speed' compression (rider movements and pedalling forces) or for 'high speed' compression (rocks and other sharp bumps). This all helps isolate rider movements from the lumps and bumps on the ground, and can cure many 'bad habits' of suspension bikes.

Travel adjustments

Most rear suspension travel changes are accomplished by moving the position of the shock in the frame. However, both Fox and RockShox, and no doubt others fairly soon, make shocks which change their travel with a flick of a switch or the turn of a dial. They're an excellent match for travel-adjustable forks.

Custom shocks

As well as all the adjustments you can make yourself, shocks can often be modified internally to change their character more dramatically and create a perfect ride for you and your bike. Due to the experience and special knowledge required and the complexity (and often pressurised parts) of the internals and the need for extreme cleanliness this is best left to professional fork servicing technicians.

Sizing

It's important to realise that shocks come in a wide range of shapes and sizes to suit different bikes. Crucial dimensions are stroke length (the actual distance the shock can compress), eye to eye length (the length from shock mount to shock mount), and the width of the spacers needed to fit the frame mount at either end.

Maintenance

Shocks are complex pieces of kit. Apart from simple cleaning, servicing and annual oil changes are best left to professional technicians.

Most lightweight, full suspension frames use air shocks with external adjustment dials/levers.

Basic frame materials

The basic building material of the mountain bike has undergone a total change during the last ten years. The use of oversized aluminium alloy tubes that was pioneered in the exotic hand-built American bikes of Klein and Cannondale is now the norm, right down to the basic £200 bike level. Steel is now the choice of a pedigree minority plus, at the other extreme, absolute beginner bikes. But what is the truth behind the hype and is alloy your ally or steel the real deal?

Material gains

There are several reasons for the change. Firstly, the technology needed for mass fabrication of aluminium frames was rapidly developed by the new bike manufacturing epicentre of the Far East. This became a way to gain access to the traditionally steel dominated market place.

Aluminium-framed bikes became more affordable. The big tubes and low weight immediately found favour with the expanding MTB market. The same manufacturers also rapidly borrowed technology from the top-end American manufacturers. By bending and thinly 'butting' tubes they soothed the inherent harshness and brutal ride delivered by aluminium. The rise of the suspension fork made ground shock less of an issue.

More recently, full suspension has demanded stiff but lightweight and often complex shaped frames to keep independently sprung wheels in line and under control. Again aluminium is ideal.

Steel

Steel was the leading bike material for over a century. The latest steel alloys such as Reynolds 853 are highly advanced materials that actually harden when welded. This enables frame weight to be more competitive with alu frames. But the real strength of steel is in its supple, springy ride quality, making it a top choice for skilful cross country hardtails.

A more gradual failure profile than alu, plus resilience and mendability are also finding it new friends in the hardnut jump and downhill arenas.

Steel also survives on low budget bikes, providing a smoother ride feel than most cheap alu framed bikes. But look for quality 'Cro-moly' steel frames rather than the thumping gas pipe feel of 'Hi-Tensile' steel.

Consider steel frames for:
- A lively 'springy' ride.
- Surviving regularly slammed aerial adventures.
- Sticking fridge magnets to your frame.

What does it all mean?

So what's the truth behind those fancy frame stickers?

- **TIG welding** Lightweight alu needs to be welded without the join being contaminated by oxygen, or it will actually catch fire. A Tungsten electrode works in a flood of the inert gas Argon to keep air out of the welding area.
- **Butting** Often seen on frame stickers, 'butted tubes' are reduced in thickness in the centre section for lightness while the ends are thicker for stronger welds. 'Single butted' tubes change thickness at one end, 'double butted' tubes change at both ends while 'taper butts' reduce thickness in stages or gradually. 'Custom butted' can mean anything (or nothing) at all.
- **Profiling** Round tubes give equal strength and stiffness in all directions, but by increasing dimensions in one particular direction you can increase stiffness and strength too. Tall 'tubes' (ovals, teardrops or rectangles) increase vertical stiffness (and allow bigger logos). Sideways ovals or rectangles increase sideways stiffness. Square tubes make welding easy, allow external machining and look butch.
- **Heat treating** This is the process of baking alu frames to harden the metal to its full strength. It's often seen as a 'T' number suffix, eg 6061-T6 on a badge.
- **Monocoques** This is a 'one piece' structure usually formed by welding two shaped alu halves together to form a light, stiff frame. It's ideal for the shapes demanded by some suspension systems but it can echo loudly off-road.

- **Hydroforming** Liquid formed aluminium tubes have recently started to change both the looks and the strength and ride characteristics of alu frames. Thicker tube walls at particular points and unusually 'swoopy' shapes can all be built into frame structures without needing to add a collection of gussets for reinforcement.

Aluminium

Aluminium is roughly one third the weight of steel, but also one third the stiffness and strength. This made early alu frames light but rather floppy and fragile affairs. The revolution came when builders abandoned the traditional diameters of steel frames to use thin walled oversized tubes to increase the strength and stiffness without increasing weight.

The real joy of alu for builders is the fact that it's so easy to play with. Stretch it or squeeze it into different shapes, cast it, forge it, or just sculpt complicated bits out of a big billet block. It's the Plasticine of metals. It allows tubes to be shaped and thickened to respond to very specific stresses within bike frames, enabling builders to tune the strength and ride of their frames very accurately.

The only major problem is the sudden failure mode of alu. If you don't leave enough of it where it's needed it'll snap without warning. A more secondary concern is that it's difficult – in fact often impossible – to repair, modify or add bits (like disc brake mounts) to alu frames.

Consider aluminium frames for:
- A sharp crisp ride feel.
- High value and reasonable weight.
- High price and ultra low weight.
- Awkward shaped suspension frames, fat tubes, big box monocoques and novelty machined sections.

Material properties can lend themselves to the overall characteristics of a bike.

Exotic materials

While the majority of mountain bikes are now crafted from alu, there are several other 'space age' materials vying for attention.
But what do they offer when they're woven, welded or cast into bike style shapes?

High tech materials, even super-costly and super-strong steels like Reynolds 953, are increasingly finding their way onto the MTB market.

Titanium

Titanium is the hardest metal for bike manufacturers to work with, but it has developed a cult and reverential following for its resilient long-term strength, light weight and corrosion resistance. This makes it an almost perfect material for cross country hardtails, but there's one big issue. Because it's so difficult and time consuming to work with, even the cheapest Ti frames can cost five times the price of an alu frame with similar butting and tube shaping features.

Shaping difficulties also make Ti unsuitable for many suspension frame designs. The future lies with pushing the boundaries of Ti manipulation and selling to a few privileged and discerning buyers. Meanwhile, the rest of us will have to rely on companies who replicate many of the ride and build features at a far lower cost.

Consider titanium frames for:
- Their resilient 'sprung' feel.
- Low weight and high strength.
- No paint or rust worries.
- You want a frame for life.

Magnesium

Magnesium is an ultralight but very volatile metal. It appeared widely as 'the new featherweight frame material' a few years ago thanks to Soviet bloc defence industry technology looking for a new home when the Cold War ended. As well as minimal weight it also benefits from high frequency damping characteristics for a silky smooth ride.

Magnesium alloys have been widely used for cast parts, like suspension fork legs, for a while now, but predictable strength in weldable tubular structures such as frames has always been an issue on large production runs and some alloys can corrode spectacularly in damp climates.

Consider magnesium frames for:
- Ultra low weight.
- Smooth riding.
- Rarity appeal.
- Highly flammable frame shavings for starting camp fires.

Carbon

Carbon, or to be more accurate carbon composite material, is popular in no-expense-spared aerospace and car racing circles. Carbon composites are essentially cloths of ultra strong threads locked into position with resin. This is then layered in sheets of different directional weaves to produce tubes or large monocoques, making it suitable for conventional hardtail or complex suspension bikes' shapes.

Carbon fibre is potentially the lightest, the strongest and most shock absorbent frame material available. However, exacting quality control and manufacturing issues mean it'll never be cheap.

Early breakages initially marred its reputation in frame building, but three major manufacturers are restoring confidence at the moment. In the componentry world, Easton's handlebars and seat posts have been big faith healers, while in the world of frame manufacture Trek have added strength and stiffness with their OCLV (Optimum Compaction Low Void) HC (HoneyComb) sandwich, and Scott's long, thick fibre 'Strike' frames have set new weight targets. New mouldable carbon technologies could open up a whole new range of complex moulded shape possibilities too.

Consider carbon frames for:
- Ultra low weight.
- If you don't mind the damped, slightly dull feel.
- If you like that black, hand knitted look.
- If holding metal frames makes your hands cold.

RAD, Zirconium, M5, Metal Matrix, Scandium

Like shampoo, aluminium has been blessed with many premium priced additives with amazing claims made for them. We're not going to argue with the claims of eminent metallurgists here, but most 'named' alloys only use a tiny amount of the material whose name they've taken. This is alloyed with standard 6000 or 7000 series aluminium to boost its performance in a particular way.

Metal Matrix and then Scandium alloys were developed for extremely high strength profiles in things like missile fins. They were adopted by bike builders as a way of lowering weight while increasing strength. However, the metals were very hard to work with and shape, so the next breed of alloys appeared. Easton 'Rad', Trek's 'Zirconium' and Specialized 'M5' alloys are all designed to make alu easier to form into complicated taper butted and twisted shapes. They put metal just where it's needed and nowhere else, enabling the designers to build lightweight frames with carefully worked out ride characters.

This kind of tweaking will always carry on, and will always carry a big price premium. Don't be at all surprised if the manufacturers contradict themselves, or each other, from one year to another. Ride before you buy and see if the reality matches the hype.

Consider spanky alu frames for:
- The latest tube shapes and alu technology.
- Daft hype names.

Carbon composites are even making their way onto top end components, but only if you're prepared to pay a lot!

Old favourites, like this GT Zaskar, are now being recreated in carbon composites.

Extra features

We've talked about frame designs, materials and suspension, but what about the other tricks of the trade that you need to pay attention to? Which 'special features' are pure hype and which offer real advantages that you'll come to love? Here's our guide to deciphering bike catalogue and sales speak...

Bottle and carrier bosses

Since suspension came on the scene bottle mountings have appeared in some bizarre places. Down tubes and seat tubes make the most sense as seat post and bottom bracket mounts just get covered in filth.

Some frames will also have bolts, or at least the threaded holes, for mounting a rear carrier rack. These are a lot more secure than clip-on extras, so look out for them if you might use rear panniers or a child seat at some point.

Even if you're not using the bottle or rack bolts, grease them so that they don't seize as they're often surprisingly useful to replace other bolts in emergencies.

Disc brake ready

Most modern MTB frames now come with disc brake mounts, either a two bolt 'International' standard B-shaped tab or, normally on forks but more unusually on frames, 'Post Mounts', which are bolt holes directly set into the chainstay. You can buy adaptors.

For real disc brake readiness, you'll also need wheels with disc hubs to fit the rotors to. Changing hubs is a major expense. Finally, check that your frame has guides to keep the hose/cable neat as it stretches from brake to handlebar lever.

The alternative is to use zip ties or extra clips.

Accessory excess?

If you ever need proof of how popular mountain biking is, go into a bike shop and see how many bits and pieces are clamouring to be bolted on for the ride.

Bells seem like a simple, light and non-aggressive way to get noticed, but don't necessarily expect walkers to hear or acknowledge them. It's a Catch 22 situation. Some people will moan if you don't ring a bell, some will moan if you do.

Bike computers range from simple speed and distance measurers to the sort of laptop style complexity that'll record every bit of ride data and bodily function information.

Fenders, or mudguards, keep you and your bike clean. They either look 'Moto' or distinctly uncool, depending on your point of view, but there's no doubting their usefulness on muddy trails in wet weather. Neoprene suspension, headset and seat post boots are also available to keep your bike's vulnerable bits happy in winter.

MTB-specific mudguards, like the Crudcatcher/ Crudguard, are an essential purchase if you ride in wet climates, like in the UK.

Blues from your bolts

Considering their small size, it's amazing how often the various bolts on your bike are the source of riding grief, in the form of niggly rattles, or lost time looking for them in bushes or under fridges. Check they're all present and well adjusted on a regular basis before they decide to turn to sabotage to get noticed.

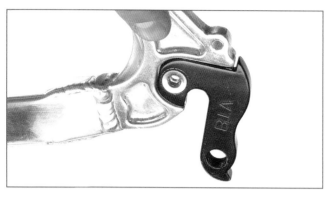

Replaceable gear hanger

An essential on aluminium frames (steel frames can usually be heated and bent back), the replaceable gear hanger is your rear gear martyr. It will snap or bend before your rear gear does in the event of an impact. You'll still be walking home, but replacement is a whole lot cheaper.

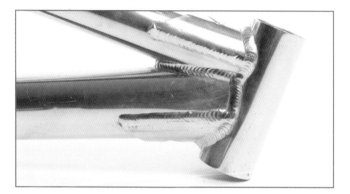

Gussets

Gussets are extra metal plates welded onto frame junctions to help spread the stress. You'll often find them tucked under the 'chin' of the bike, between the head tube and the downtube. The more abuse the bike is designed to take the more they'll appear in other places. Regard them as external butting, or buttressing.

Headsets

Traditionally, steering bearings sat in cups that were hammered into the head tube of the frame. More recently, manufacturers realised that by just creating the frame to allow direct fitting of the bearings they save the extra weight and hassle of the hammer-in cups.

Big tyre clearance

It's taken some manufacturers a while to work this out, but having lots of room around tyres is essential to keep them turning if they're caked in sticky mud. Big tyre clearances also let you fit big stout tyres that can handle rocky trails and crashed landings without bursting. Always check the mudroom at all points though, as clearance is only as big as the smallest gap.

Dropped or sloping top tubes

Top tubes – or 'crossbars' – that slope downward started appearing on Canadian bikes long ago. These days they're pretty much universal. The sloping top tube offers more clearance between your most sensitive parts and the frame, so if you have to jump off suddenly you're less likely to hurt yourself. It also makes the frame stiffer and lighter, as it makes for a more compact triangle structure.

Getting the right size

You can have all the fancy frame materials or suspension systems you want on your new bike, but you won't enjoy riding it unless it's the right size and shape for you and the riding you do.

Joining the dots

There are still people out there who will tell you that a bike fits right when 'you can touch the ground with the balls of both feet when you're sat in the saddle'. For the purposes of getting maximum enjoyment out of your bike, this advice is best forgotten.

Most of the following advice is based on conventional 'diamond' frames, but even unconventional frames, with bits missing or extra bits bolted on, all use the same basic dimensions and angles. They simply join the dots in different ways. If there isn't a top tube, measure the distance from the seat post to the stem. If there isn't a seat tube, measure the distance from the top of the seat post holding tube to the centre of the bottom bracket for equivalent measurements.

Height

For maximum power output your leg should be straight when you're sat on the saddle with your heel resting on the pedal at its lowest point. If the saddle is too low, your muscles aren't being used efficiently. If it's too high, you'll be rocking your pelvis to either side as you pedal, which will give you back ache. See our 'Technique' chapter for more details.

A quick look around will reveal a lot of riders panting about with their knees up around their ears and the saddle as low as it can go. The idea here is that lowering the seat out of the way leaves the rider freer to shift bodyweight about for control when jumping or tackling extreme terrain. You'll know where you're riding priorities lie, but if you want to have an option of pedalling efficiency or maximum control as terrain dictates, then pick a frame with a quick release seat post so that you can drop the saddle in seconds.

Length

If you can get the saddle high enough for an 'efficient' pedalling position without pushing the seat post above its maximum mark (most will have a 'Max' mark on them) then a bike is probably about the right length for general riding too. However, different tricks require different dogs.

Long bikes that stretch the rider out are great for cross country power riding but harder to flick around or shift your bodyweight about on tight singletrack or jumps. Short bikes that can be thrown around leave the rider feeling cramped and sat upright for long hauls. Again, if you have specific riding priorities choose a frame slightly larger or smaller than normal to suit. Any frame is a compromise if you're riding terrain that it wasn't designed for.

As well as top tube length, the length of the rear section of the bike is important too. The longer the chainstays the more stable and forgiving the bike will be. The shorter they are the quicker it will accelerate and turn but the harsher it will feel over rough terrain. Most bikes are very similar in this dimension due to a desire for balanced handling and due to practical problems such as tyre clearance on short seatstay bikes.

Longer travel suspension bikes need a longer back end to give room for the wheel travel, and use a shorter front end to compensate. Other bikes use a short back end for direct power application, combined with a longer top tube to keep the wheelbase, and therefore stability, similar to conventional frames. Finally, some bikes use unusual seat angles that change the saddle to handlebar reach significantly as you raise/lower the post. Bear in mind that you can change the seat position slightly by sliding the saddle back and forth on its rails.

Geometry

As well as the length dimensions of the bike, the angles of the tubes are crucial too. Most bikes have an active geometry of around 71 degrees for the head angle and 73 degrees for the seat angle. This makes for a frame that's responsive without feeling nervous in tight situations. Static angles (before you climb on the bike) will usually be a little different, as suspension sag has to be taken into account.

The biggest deviations from these magic figures occur on downhill or slalom bikes, where the angles are often slackened by several degrees to give more stable handling at high speeds. The resulting slower steering is countered with shorter stems and wider bars for leverage.

It's also worth pointing out that while most frames are now designed to take a suspension fork with 100mm plus of travel, adding a longer fork than the bike was designed for will tilt the bike back, slacken the angles and make the steering slower. Conversely, fitting a shorter fork will steepen the angles and quicken the steering.

If the bike doesn't fit, your energy is wasted and your enjoyment diminished. It's a bit like buying the wrong size shoes – even if you spent a lot of money on them they're useless unless they fit properly and will ultimately cause you pain and suffering!

Every seat post has a 'maximum' height line.

CHAPTER 6

Bike anatomy – components

If you've read the previous chapter, you should know all there is to know about the frame and forks. But what about the rest of the bike? It's easy to overlook the importance of all those unsung componentry heroes. Your comfort, attitude and latent riding skills are all substantially affected by all the bits and pieces fastened to your frame. All those interactive contact points that link you with your bike and the ground are there to ensure your constantly happy and fulfilling relationship with the bike. Careful selection and knowledge of your component parts is every bit as important as careful selection and knowledge of your frame and forks.

The XTR crank from Shimano is one of the most evolved components, addressing every element of performance in achieving a balance of weight and stiffness.

As mountain biking has become more extreme, brakes have had to step up to new demands for power and control. Disc brakes are now commonplace on most mid- to top-end MTBs.

Headsets and bottom brackets

The bottom bracket

Lurking almost unnoticed in the bowels of your bike, the bottom bracket is one of the most heavily stressed yet overlooked components on a bike. Here's what you need to know about this hidden hero...

Materials

Bottom bracket axles can be made from steel or titanium. Steel is the norm. It's cheap, stiff and not prone to flexing or squeaking. Titanium axles have been known to flex or creak slightly in high load situations, but their lighter weight makes them popular with racers.

Bearings

Old-style bottom brackets involved an axle, screw-in cups, and two sets of bearings, all easily serviced and bearings easily replaced. Sealed 'fit and forget' cartridge units then became the norm. Top-end bike makers are now fitting simple, often oversized, press-fit bearings that can be refurbished when the original parts wear out.

Different turns

Splined (or toothed) bottom bracket axles give more rigid and reliable contact. They're lighter and are gradually replacing traditional square axles. Unfortunately Shimano's Octalink cranks use one standard while other cranks use a different (ISIS) standard. Meanwhile other three-piece cranks such as Profile and XTR use their own specific splined axles.

Bombproofing

As well as splined or square bottom bracket axles there are some heavy-duty chainsets that use axles with the crankarms welded or bolted into place at one or both ends. Though these units are generally stiffer and stronger they are also much heavier.

Popular cartridge type bottom bracket units showing top end square taper axles (above) and ISIS splined (below)'.

External bearing bottom bracket cups are becoming the norm on top-end bikes now, as are single-piece crank and axle assemblies.

Headsets

The headset is responsible for letting you steer safely and with control through the trials and tribulations of trails. It's arguably the most important bearing on your bike.

Getting Ahead?

Although they're known as headsets, most steering bearings are actually licensed versions of Dia Compe's 'Aheadset' system. This non-threaded push-fit system uses a smooth steerer with bearings and spacers that slide into place. The Aheadset stem then clamps around the steerer tube and the whole lot is held in place with a top cap that presses down onto the top of the stem via a bolt into a starfangled nut inside the headtube.

The Integrated Aheadset system trims weight further, especially when compared to the traditional threaded headset, by setting bearing races directly into the frame rather than into extra push-in cups.

Some older or low cost bikes still use a threaded headset/steerer with a stem that plugs inside. They're a bit heavier and not as mechanically efficient, but the stems offer easy height adjustment.

Check the headtube size of your frame. Older or low-budget bikes are often 1in in diameter, but most modern frames are 1.125in. Heavy-duty bikes sometimes use a larger 1.5in standard, and some manufacturers are now using 1.125in upper bearings and 1.5in lower.

You pays your money...

Although headsets are relatively simple devices, there's a wide range of prices depending on quality of bearings and the quality of the seals that protect them. While some headsets last for a matter of months if they're ridden hard, others like Chris King's legendary units can last for years and will move from bike to bike as frames or forks are replaced.

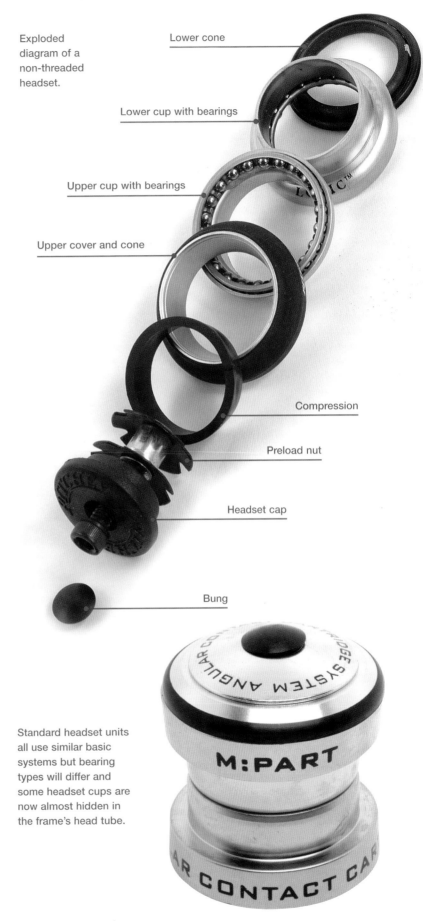

Exploded diagram of a non-threaded headset.

Lower cone

Lower cup with bearings

Upper cup with bearings

Upper cover and cone

Compression

Preload nut

Headset cap

Bung

Standard headset units all use similar basic systems but bearing types will differ and some headset cups are now almost hidden in the frame's head tube.

The cockpit

Stems, handlebars and grips are a vital contact point with your bike, and can define a lot of its ride and handling character.

Stems

Outwardly, a stem is a simple piece of metal with a handlebar clamped in one end and the fork steerer clamped in the other, but the design and size of your stem has a massive effect on your bike's handling and fit.

A long stem pushes rider weight forward and increases the inertia of the steering for stable steering as well as giving room for the rider to stretch out and breathe.

Shorter stems move rider weight back. This makes the steering and the whole front end of the bike feel very light. The bike can be steered very quickly, but with less weight up front the wheel will lift on climbs or wash out in corners unless rider weight is deliberately pushed forward. As shorter stems are often used with longer travel forks, it makes a lot of sense to ride with your weight a bit further forward.

Handlebars

'Wavey' shaped riser bars are becoming the universal MTB norm these days. And it's not all just down to fashion. Wider, higher handlebars are a big boost to comfort and handling on difficult terrain.

The wider the bar, the bigger the leverage on the steering and the more control the rider has, whether it's in subtle technical riding moments or when hammering through rocks at high speed. A wide bar (24in plus) also opens up the rider's chest cavity for more efficient breathing. Many riders find that the back-sweep of a typical riser bar also puts hands

and wrists in a more comfy position. The downside of wide riser bars is that they're heavier than skinny flatter bars, and there comes a point where they'll no longer fit between trees. Also, if you have skinny shoulders they may just stretch your arms too far apart for comfort.

Narrow bars (22 inches or less) are lighter but they reduce leverage, making control inputs heavy. They're fine at speed over less demanding terrain, but feel lurchy and unsubtle at low speeds compared to risers.

As with other components, more expensive bars get either lighter or stronger, depending on your priorities. Carbon handlebars are becoming increasingly popular by combining both attributes.

Grips

Grips are a surprisingly important aspect of how your bike feels. Most manufacturers are clued up to this now, and factory-fit decent grips. But sooner or later they will wear out, or perhaps you'll just want to try something different. Soft-surfaced lumpy pattern or ribbed 'mushroom' grips give massive grip and comfort while thin hard grips give the most trail feedback. Dual compound grips give the best of both worlds.

The cheapest grips are basic rubber bar covers, or cheap foam, while you will get durable, comfy, dual compound or light foam grips in loads of colours, sizes and styles for a very small amount of money. The most expensive grips use aluminium clamp rings on the outside of the rubber section to stop them spinning or slipping.

The rider's nerve centre. From here you handle all the steering, braking and gear selection.

Some brake and gear levers are combined units. Others, like this, allow you to choose separate brand brakes and gears.

Saddles and seat posts

As your contact point at the far end of the bike, saddles and seatposts don't change handling as much as your cockpit, but they definitely have a big effect on comfort, which obviously affects the feel-good factor of your bike and what you're getting out of it.

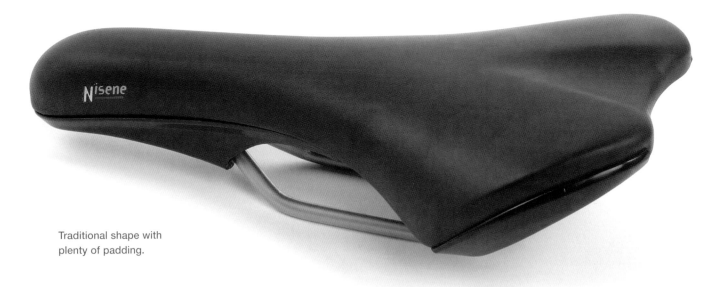

Traditional shape with plenty of padding.

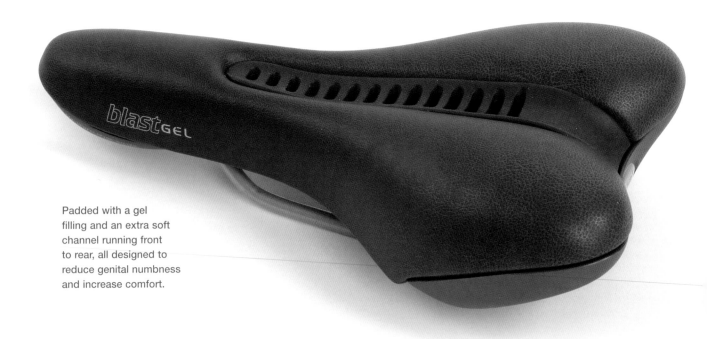

Padded with a gel filling and an extra soft channel running front to rear, all designed to reduce genital numbness and increase comfort.

Saddles

Everyone's seating preferences and riding habits are different. There's a saddle out there for everyone (plus a few that defy reason).

Big saddles tend to give lots of weight placement positions and comfort control. Narrow saddles are light, they don't get in the way of pedalling but they take a bit of getting used to. Then there's a whole range of soft centres or gaping holes to fight the overhyped impotence issue.

Saddle tops are available in every colour you can think of. Leather rules for comfort and durability, embroidery looks fast, while tough Kevlar side panels are great for preventing unsightly scuffs, but can destroy your shorts. The lightest saddles of all are carbon shelled, but fragility and no padding means they're not recommended for anyone but racers.

Thick padding might seem like a good idea, but on longer rides it'll make you sweatier and cause saddle soreness. Think thin but firm for riding distances.

The rails underneath saddles might be solid steel, tubular steel alloy or titanium, each getting progressively lighter and more costly. Titanium rails give a natural spring to the seat, but some saddles achieve this on a lower budget by using little rubber bungs between the rails and the saddle for shock absorption.

Seat posts

A seat post is quite simply a tube to hold your seat at the right height above the frame, but it's available in many flavours and designs.

Surprisingly, there are few specially built heavy-duty posts for hardnut riding, probably because such riders usually have their saddles pushed way down and out of the way. If you're after strength, think thick and heavy. Otherwise the more you pay the lighter your post will be, usually without losing strength.

Replacement posts need to be exactly the same size as the bike frame, right down to fractions of a millimetre. Check what post you took out and match it with your new one. Also check whether the clamp holding the saddle is in line or with a slight 'layback' as this can affect your riding position. A 'layback' clamp can effectively add an inch or so to your stretch to the bars.

Finally, make sure it's long enough to give you the right saddle height, without extending beyond its 'Maximum' extension mark (or 'Minimum' insertion mark), otherwise it might bend or break, or do the same to your frame. Always make sure there's at least 2 inches of post inside the main triangle of the frame.

The cheapest seat posts are steel, which is heavy and jarring to ride on. Alu posts range from humble plain pipe up to ultralight custom posts. If you're really weight watching, titanium and carbon fibre seatposts are superlight, and both offer excellent resilient damping characteristics for extra comfort.

If you're looking for extra comfort on a hardtail frame, consider getting a suspension seatpost. The shorter travel telescopic ones are the most common, but the more costly parallelogram ones can offer up to 4 inches of plush travel. They're a cheap alternative to a full suspension frame.

Sensitive issues

There has been a lot of hype about male impotence and cycling, but it's generally agreed that the massive cardiovascular benefits of cycling on virility greatly outweigh the tiny possibility for problems.

From the female angle, a woman's pelvic bone structure is significantly wider, with a bigger gap between the sit bones, so women's saddles are built wider to support the right places. Noses of women's saddles will also generally be shorter or centrally cut away to reduce pressure on softer parts if you crouch forward.

A good women's saddle will feature a cutaway channel, extra padding and will be ergonomically designed for the female form.

A seat post can be both light and strong with the use of modern materials such as carbon fibre.

Rims and tyres

Rims

Rims are the essential rolling stock on your bike. All decent rims are made of aluminium alloys. The old-school low budget steel rims have a legendary lack of stopping power. Various shapes and widths exist for a wide range of rolling roles but as a general rule the wider and deeper the rim the stronger it will be. Ultralight XC rims might be sub 400g, downhill rims might be anything up to double that.

Rims are pre-drilled for a certain number of spokes. 32 spokes is the norm but lightweight front rims may go as low as 24 spokes and tandem wheels may have as many as 40. Finding replacement rims and hubs for anything but 28, 32, and 36 can be a major problem though.

Special needs

The sidewalls of most good rims are machined flat for consistent brake surfaces without a notch at the welded join. Some rims also use hard, high-friction coatings.

You can avoid wearing your rims through heavy braking by running disc brakes. Special disc-specific rims without braking surfaces are now common, and many are lighter than rims with braking surfaces.

Tubeless tyres require dedicated airtight rims to create a complete tyre seal. They're more expensive but they'll handle a standard tyre and tube set-up if you change your mind. Some enthusiasts are now using liquid tyre sealants, like latex, instead of inner tubes.

Disc specific rims (top) do away with tall braking surfaces on the sides and therefore can be shaped for stength alone. This often results in lower weights. Choose your tyres and rims wisely, as less rotating weight and faster tread profiles will noticably increase speed.

Tyres

They're round, they're usually made from rubber and they're crucial to how well your bike sticks to the ground.

Getting a grip

With few exceptions more grip equals more drag. Big chunky knobs dig in better, but the bigger the knobs, the more space you'll need between them to clear mud. Lower, closer spaced knobs roll faster on dry trails. Tyres with slick centres are the fastest but sketchiest of all. Softer compounds give better grip in hard conditions, but wear quickly. Cheap, hard tyres last for ever but won't grip as well.

Size – it is important

The larger a tyre, the more air is between the ground and the rim. 1.9 to 2.1 inch tyres are a happy medium between weight and protection for most purposes. Bigger tyres (2.3 to 3 inch) can be run softer for better traction, with less risk of pinch punctures, but they are hard to accelerate. 1.5 to 1.8 inch lightweight cross country race tyres accelerate fast but need high pressures to survive rocky terrain, and they're a harsh ride.

Special powers

Folding or Kevlar beads make tyres lighter but more expensive. Some tyres have thorn protection layers under the tread or anti-pinch flat strips above the bead. Most seem to work to a degree, so if you're having particular problems in these areas, try them out. Tubeless tyres eliminate the need for an inner tube and survive pinch flats far better. They also give a really smooth 'floaty' feel, but they're expensive and need special rims and repair kits. Many riders choose to run liquid latex based kits, with special rim tapes, that convert normal wheels and tyres to tubeless. And many manufacturers now make 'Tubeless Ready' tyres, specifically for use with liquid sealants to prevent air loss.

It's important to think about tyre tread width, height and profile. Different types suit different terrain. High profile knobs (left) will grip better in mud but roll slower, while a lower profile centre tread (right) will roll faster but be less grippy in mud.

Hubs and spokes

A metal tube full of bearings and a few steel strings might not sound very exciting but your hub and spokes are literally central to the speed and handling performance of your bike.

Hubs

Hubs are basically a tube with raised flanges for spokes to be threaded through, and with bearings at either end to support the axle. Hubs are available in different spoke-hole drillings, typically 32, but 28 and 36 are relatively common and specialist applications use spoking patterns anywhere from 16 to 48 to match different rims and users.

Most hubs use sealed cartridge bearings which can be replaced if they start to wobble. Some hubs use cones and bearings that can be serviced and might last longer. The majority of hubs use a quick-release lever to fasten them in place, but for extra stiffness on heavier-duty bikes oversize axles that bolt into the dropouts are becoming increasingly common. If you want to run disc brakes, you'll need hubs that the rotors can be fixed to. Most use six bolt holes around the hub flange, but some (such as Shimano centre-lock hubs) use other fastening systems.

Other options

Internal hub gears have the big advantages of sealed mechanism and single chainline but they suffer from massive weight.

As you'd expect, singlespeed hubs are built specially for single geared MTBs – a growing niche in both the cross country and jump scenes.

Hubs are an important component in making your bike roll freely.

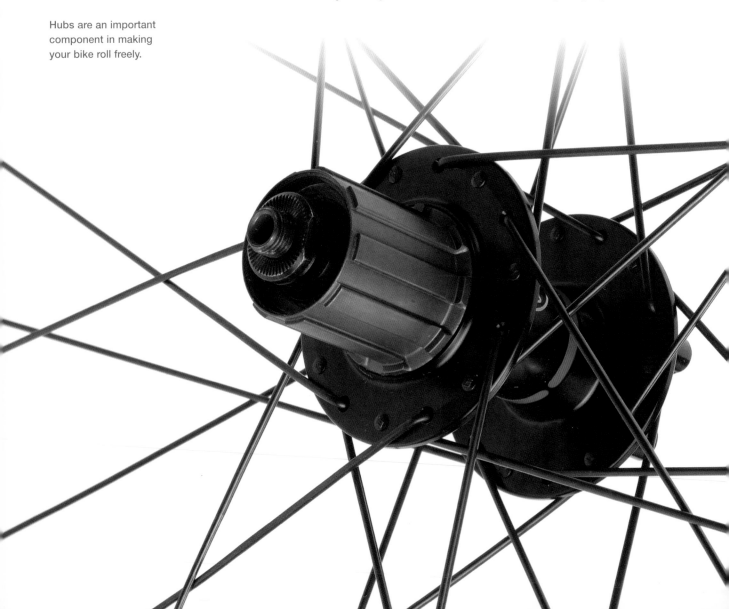

Spokes

Spokes are generally stainless steel, which resists rust and tensions well, but titanium, metal matrix, aluminium and even Kevlar string are used in some wheelsets.

The more spokes, the wider the loads are spread, but the more metal and weight you're using. Most wheels use 32 spokes, but heavyweight applications can use 36 or even 40 to spread the load, while delicate lightweight front wheels might have as few as 16 spokes.

Spokes are available in different wire 'gauges' (thickness) ranging from 12 (super strong for downhill and tandems) to 17 gauge (ultralight race spokes). For most purposes 13 or 14 gauge is spot on. Top quality spoke designs are butted (changed in thickness) to reduce weight in the centre where stress is lower. Some are single butted at the hub end, others are double butted at both ends. Spoke lengths also differ according to hub, rim and lacing patterns, so take the wheel in if you need a replacement.

Wheelsets

Complete ready-to-ride wheelsets are becoming increasingly popular as an upgrade purchase. They range from cheap and cheerful to super-light carbon-rimmed race wheels. The supposed advantages of the high-tech wheels are reduced weight and/or increased strength, as well as great looks. However, non-standard components on some of these wheels will often mean wheels need returning to the manufacturer for repair, and comparative testing shows that few of them are lighter or tougher than a standard high-quality wheelbuild.

Buying ready-to-ride wheelsets has its advantages when chosen carefully, though many riders still choose to have their wheels custom built at their local bike shop.

Cranksets and pedals

Cranks

Cranks are the cunning levers that turn your stamping feet in a smooth circular motion. Without cranks your bike is just a big scooter.

Shapes

Cranks come in all sorts of shapes, from rectangular monoliths to thin tubes, and everything in between. Basically material on the outer edges gives more strength and stiffness while the centre is under much less stress. This is why many cranks have hollow backs, while Shimano have developed cranks with a hollow centre.

Shimano design some of their cranks to run on splined axles, which are generally stronger, lighter and stiffer than square tapered axles. Others use the slightly different (licensing reasons) ISIS splined system. Older cranks still use simple square tapered axles.

Weights vary greatly depending on price and purpose. Chunky three-piece welded Cro Mo steel downhill/jump bike cranks might weigh well over a kilo, while superlight alu or carbon-wrap cranks are often under 700g.

Pick your crankarms depending on the level of abuse you give your bike. Most cranks are 175mm. Shorter legged riders should hunt out 170, even 165mm lengths, but long limbed riders and big gear pushers might enjoy the extra leverage of 180mm cranks.

Chainrings

Most bikes use a triple chainset with three rings for a wide spread of gears. Ring sizes are typically 44 or 42 tooth on the outside, 32 tooth in the middle and 22 tooth on the inside, often called the 'granny' ring.

Some racers prefer to use a double chainset (normally 42 tooth outer, 29 or 30 tooth inner) while 'Freeriders' might use the same set-up with a protective guard in place of the outer ring. Downhill, jump, trials and singlespeed bikes just use a single chainring.

Pedals

There are masses of pedal types, but which ones are right for you?

Mountain bikers and their pedals tend to be split into two camps. Riders who like to lock their feet in place for maximum pedal power generally use 'clipless' pedals, which work very much like 'step in, twist out' ski bindings. These are nearly all based on Shimano's SPD (or 'SpuD') design, although Time pedals are also popular and there are other alternatives too. You'll need special 'SPD compatible' shoes to use such pedals.

Many downhill, jump, trials or slalom racers like to get off the bike as fast as possible for certain moves (or in crashes) and prefer to use soft soled shoes and big studded 'platform' pedals. Halfway between the two extremes are pedals with clip-in centres surrounded by platform cages, which work in any situation with either type of shoe.

Many beginners prefer to use platform pedals to start with, and many riders still like the old-school clips and straps option, which lets you bind your feet to the pedals without having to buy special shoes.

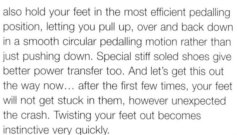

Why clipless?

Clipless pedals are a major power efficiency advantage if cross country riding over serious terrain. They keep your feet from bouncing off your pedals on rough ground and they make it a lot easier to lift the bike up off the ground to clear obstacles. They also hold your feet in the most efficient pedalling position, letting you pull up, over and back down in a smooth circular pedalling motion rather than just pushing down. Special stiff soled shoes give better power transfer too. And let's get this out the way now... after the first few times, your feet will not get stuck in them, however unexpected the crash. Twisting your feet out becomes instinctive very quickly.

A clipless pedal with a moulded body keeps your feet in position on the pedal even when not properly clipped in.

State of the art, minimalist and super lightweight clipless pedal. Ideal for racers.

Reversible clipless pedal with cast body. Will suit anyone wanting to give clipless a go.

Traditional/old-school clips and straps don't require special footwear.

Cassettes and chains

The simple chain and cog mechanism that drives
your bike is primitive, but it's also an incredibly
efficient transmission system.
What do you need to know
to keep it that way?

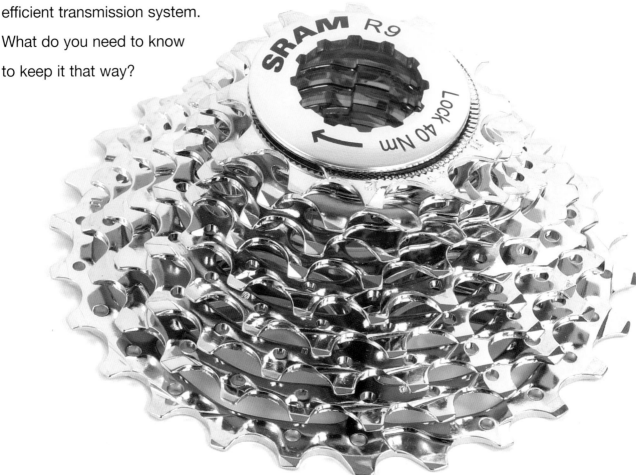

The cassette

Sometimes referred to as a 'block' or freewheel, the
cassette is the collection of cogs, sometimes called
sprockets, that sits on your rear wheel to keep your
knees turning at the appropriate rate whatever the trail
is doing.

Sizes

By using multiple gears your mountain bike can tackle
any terrain. The larger the sprocket is on the cassette,
the easier the gear is to push. To confuse matters,
this works the other way round with the chainrings at
the front. It's the smaller chainrings that make things
easier up front.

Cassettes typically use a bottom gear (biggest
cog) of 32 or 34 tooth. When used with your smallest
ring at the front this will enable you to climb almost
anything. At the opposite end, an 11 or 12 tooth
sprocket is normally fitted for high speed road work.

Nine sprockets is
now the norm on
quality MTBs.

A free hub has the
rachet in the hub and
not the gear cassette.

Shapes

Don't worry if some of the cassette cog teeth look stunted or twisted before you even use them. Different tooth shapes and angles are used to help the chain shift smoothly and quickly between one gear and the next.

7, 8 or 9 speed

Extra cogs on a cassette usually mean that the jumps between gears are slightly smaller, making for smoother progression through the gears as you speed up or slow down. The size of the biggest and smallest cogs on 7, 8 or 9 speed cassettes might vary slightly, but this makes very little difference to achievable speeds, which are more to do with attaining the right mix of strength and pedalling fluidity.

While 7 and 8 speed systems usually use the same chains and spacing, 9 speed is a law unto itself. Different chain widths and shifter spacings mean that to upgrade from 8 to 9 speed requires an almost complete replacement of parts.

Freehubs or freewheels

Freehubs keep the freewheel mechanism attached to the hub. The cogs of the cassette slide on over the top of the freehub. Freehubs are now almost universal on anything other than very low budget bikes. The cog cluster (or individual sprockets) can be replaced easily when it wears out, while the freehub lasts a lot longer.

A freewheel, on the other hand, puts the mechanism and the cogs all in one 'block', which is then screwed onto the hub. You have to replace the whole thing if it's worn.

Chains

Considering the amount of mechanical and muck abuse chains receive, they still work remarkably well. Here's what you need to know to keep your links in prime condition...

Each chain link consists of two side plates and two rollers, joined with a push-fit rivet. Most chains are supplied as 116 links, often more than you need to wrap around the biggest cog at the back and biggest ring at the front. The chain needs to be shortened with a chain splitting tool. Keep the other links as spares.

Traditionally, chains could be shortened and rejoined at any point, using the same rivet. These days, there are a few different systems. Shimano chains need a special replacement rivet, while some chains use a clever split link design to make removal and replacement tool-free.

More gears means more sprockets in the cassette and tighter spacing, so make sure you buy the right 8 or 9 speed chain for your gears.

Care and wear

Always make sure you clean and lubricate your chain after every ride. A gentle hose and scrubbing brush will work, but there are easy to use chain cleaning baths available too. Once the chain is clean, lubricate the links with a good quality chain lube. Use a sticky wet lube for winter protection and a dry Teflon-style lube to stop dust and grime collecting in summer.

Chains wear fast, especially if they're not kept clean and lubricated, so always check your links regularly. A useful gauge of chain wear is that 12 links should measure exactly 12 inches. When they measure 12.125 inches replace the chain. Otherwise replace it when it starts to slip or looks loose on the chainring otherwise you'll wear all the other bits too.

A chain breaker can remove the pins from a chain for maintenance or repair.

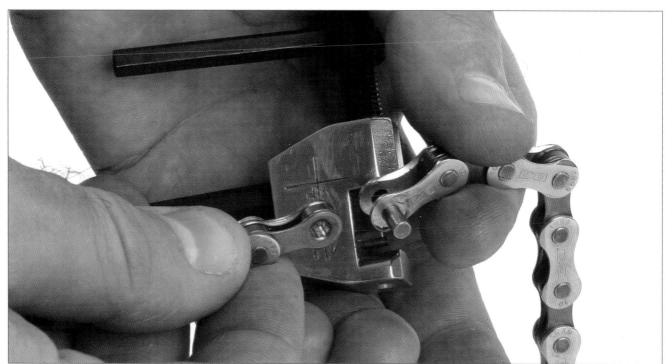

Gear mechs and shifters

The wide range of gears are what make mountain bikes such great bikes for all terrains and purposes, but how exactly does all that pushing and pulling of chains and cables control your cogs?

You can now choose from separate gear shifters and brake levers or Dual Control set-ups that incorporate the gears and brakes.

The shifters on your handlebars work by pulling just the right amount of cable to move the gear mechanisms one cog up or down. The click you hear as this happens is what's known as 'indexing'. Shifters can perform their function in a few different ways. The most dominant these days use separate up and down triggers, or a twist of the wrist (SRAM's Gripshift), but Shimano also offer a system that uses up or down movement of the brake lever. Older methods were dominated by thumbshifters that you pushed or pulled.

Which method you choose depends on personal taste and, of course, how much money you want to spend. Each style has its fans. However they do it, the right-hand shifters always control the rear gears (usually 8 or 9) while the left-hand shifter moves the chain between 3 front rings to give the full 24 or 27 ratios.

The Gripshift system. The part of the grip that rotates has an indexed gear shifter built into it.

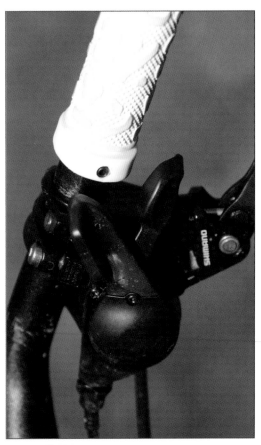

Front changer

The front gear changer (or derailleur or mech) is a shaped cage that pushes the chain up and across or down and across, literally shoving the chain from one ring to another. Although they all appear similar, more money buys better component parts for a smoother and longer life.

There are two key things to check when buying a front mech. Firstly, check that it works in the right direction for the cable routing of your bike. 'Top pull' mechs use a cable coming from above, while 'bottom pull' mechs use a cable passing underneath the bottom bracket shell. Some of the new front mechs can work either way.

You'll also need to make sure that the mounting clamp is the right size (28.6, 31.8 or 34.9mm) for the seat tube of your bike (some new mechs are one-size-fits-all via shims). If there's no seat tube (rare, but some suspension bikes don't have one) you'll need an 'E type' mech, which is mounted on special plates.

Rear changer

The rear gear changer ('derailleur' or 'mech') is a precise parallelogram device that's moved sideways, by cable pull, exactly the right distance from one cog to another. The chain itself runs over two jockey wheels carried in the cage that hangs below, which is sprung backwards to keep the chain slack in tension.

While front mechs will work with any shifter, you have to be careful to match rear mechs and shifters correctly. Most Shimano rear mechs will work happily with other Shimano shifters (7, 8 or 9 speed). The only one that causes a problem is Shimano Rapid Rise, which works in exact reverse to give racers an option of faster shifts to faster gears.

SRAM produce Shimano shifter compatible mechs, and Shimano mech compatible shifters, but SRAM-specific shifters and mechs use double the cable pull of Shimano and only work with other SRAM parts.

Rear changers also come in two different versions – standard long cage and short cage for racers using a narrower gear range.

Maintenance

Apart from keeping them clean and lightly lubricated, and adjusting the cable tension if it starts to slip, there's not much more you can do to help shifters and gears. The real secret to happy shifting is keeping cables and chains running smoothly.

Singlespeeds

The puritanical niche notion of forgetting gears altogether is becoming more and more popular. You'll be surprised how fast you can ride, and up what, on a singlespeed bike. Their simplicity makes them great winter bikes, and they've always been popular on the jump scene (like BMXes).

Left, SRAM's ESP mechs use double the cable pull of Shimano.

Right, Shimano Rapidrise gear mechanisms have the spring working to push the chain onto bigger sprockets, but most riders still choose the normal mechs.

Brakes and levers

Riding as fast as you can is great fun. But if you can't stop properly you will soon lose the smile off your face, often to a big hard tree. So what anchors are available for eyeball-popping stopping?

V brakes

V brakes was the original name given to Shimano's parallelogram action side pull cantilevers. These days most of the straight arm straight pull cantilevers are referred to as Vs too. They're the most common way to stop a mountain bike.

V type brakes use two long arms bolted onto the frame to squeeze the pads hard against the rim when you pull the cable. Their advantage is their simplicity, low cost and low weight. Their disadvantage is that, while they're more powerful than older style centre pull cantilevers, they're not as powerful as disc brakes in poor conditions. Mud or water on the wheel rims makes them weaker stoppers. The pads also wear out very quickly in winter conditions.

The best way to upgrade V type brakes is to fit metal backed 'cartridge' pads which give sharper braking, or use special ceramic coated rims.

Disc brakes are standard on almost all MTBs these days. They're more consistant stoppers than V brakes. Some entry level bikes will still have V brakes, and some riders still prefer them because they're slightly lighter and easy to home-service.

Disc brakes

Disc brakes are becoming more and more common. Good examples offer more power, more control and much better poor-conditions performance than V brakes.

By having the braking rotor at the hub, disc brakes are far less affected by mud and rim damage. The powerful direct bite of the calipers means more stopping power and the latest hydraulic disc brakes are also very close to V type brakes in terms of overall weight.

Hydraulic disc brakes

Hydraulic brakes avoid the stretch and sticking of wire cables by using oil filled hoses to connect lever and brake caliper. As a result they give the best control and reliability.

The brake fluid reservoir is part of the brake lever. On 'open' brakes the system automatically adjusts for pad wear and the heat build caused by long descents, making them the best downhill brakes. On 'closed' brakes an easily accessible dial adjusts the fluid level for exact lever reach and control. Unfortunately the fluid expansion in 'closed' brakes means that they can pump up and lock on if they get too hot.

While they may sound complex, hydraulic discs need little maintenance apart from occasional brake

pad changes. Most brakes use two hydraulic pistons (pots) pushing the pads onto each side of the rotor, but some systems use four pots (two each side). This increases both braking power and subtle brake control, but brake power is more affected by the size of the disc rotor being used. Most brakes use a 160/165mm rotor to balance weight and power, but downhillers use bigger 185, or even 205mm discs for maximum stoppage. Different systems also use different shaped pads so make sure you get the right kind of replacements.

Cable disc brakes

Cable discs have simplicity, V brake lever compatibility and lower cost on their side, but cable stretch and contamination will often mean that they're less reliable than hydraulic discs. Even the best of them are far less weatherproof than hydraulics and they usually have a less precise control feel. They're also heavier than either Vs or hydraulic discs.

Other brakes

Hydraulic rim brakes have all the wet weather disadvantages of Vs but have a more powerful and direct bite, making them very popular with trials riders.

Centre pull cantilevers are the short armed predecessors of the V type brakes. They have much less stopping power.

Top Left: Hydraulic disc brake levers are neat, light and very powerful, with the fluid reservoir in the lever body.

Bottom Left: Top end V brakes are still popular with some riders because of their lightweight simplicity.

Above: Shimano's classic XTR V brake is an effective stopper in all but the slimiest conditions, where discs get the advantage.

CHAPTER 7

Trail comfort

There are many things to consider when trying to stay comfy and prepared on the trail. Mountain bike specific clothing is getting better all the time. You can dress like an enthusiast road cyclist (as most cross country racers do) or you can also opt for more casual clothes from a wide range of excellent technically designed togs. Trends are swaying towards casual baggy, rather than figure hugging Lycra, and all the best stuff is superbly designed to look like street clothing but perform well in poor conditions. As more thought has gone into togs, the market for women specific kit has increased too. In short, being properly dressed and prepared for the task in hand has become just as important as finding the right bike.

Technical clothing doesn't always mean Lycra, more casual looking kit is increasingly popular.

Thanks to www.groundsffect.co.nz for providing the clothing and pics for this chapter.

Just like choosing the right bike, wearing the right clothes is important.

Specific clothing

The nature of mountain biking, compared to road cycling, requires a bit more performance from its clothing. The solitude of the great outdoors and fickle weather means that you need to dress appropriately for the conditions and be prepared for the worst. Venturing out in a standard sports outfit just isn't suitable for the task at hand. It pays to invest in some quality threads to get the most out of your riding.

Today's technical clothing is made from lightweight and comfortable fabrics that have been designed to offer a high level of performance. The trend is towards the casual baggy look rather than skin-tight Lycra, but both have their place depending on what type of riding you're into.

Baggy shorts and tops are designed to look like street clothing but with careful design and fabric choices they look good and perform as well as the best sports wear. You can wear baggies around town without feeling as self-conscious as you might in race-ready Lycra. The relaxed styling and freedom of the baggy look make it a favoured choice for casual rides but they perform just as well on the longer ones.

These more casual shorts usually feature an internal liner with a padded insert, much like Lycra shorts, to increase saddle comfort. The outer is specifically cut for riding, and is often made of a lightweight rip-stop material that's been designed to withstand trailside obstacles and the occasional fall. Some even feature stretch panels to improve pedalling freedom and meshed sections to increase ventilation. A few pockets are often standard and are useful for temporary storage, but not as a carrying solution.

Baggy jerseys are pretty similar to the tighter Lycra variety but in a looser fit which makes them cooler in hotter weather. Most are made from performance fabrics that are designed to wick moisture away from the skin.

The skin-tight Lycra look is what most people assume to be cycle clothing. It's a lot racier than the laid back baggy clothing and tends to be the choice of the club cycling enthusiast or racer. It's extremely versatile, can be worn all the year round and comes in various forms, depending on the conditions. The contoured fit acts like a second skin and, although it looks a little strange off the bike, it's ideal comfort wear when you're planning a long ride. The Lycra tag tends to be the generic name for any tight fit clothing, but there's a lot more to Lycra than meets the eye.

Shorts are made from panels to ensure an anatomically correct fit. They feature a high performance insert in the crotch area (this used to be made from Chamois leather but these days it will usually be man-made fibre) to increase comfort and move away sweat.

Full length thermal tights are ideal for cold riding conditions and will keep you warm through wind, rain and snow. Combine a long sleeved thermal jersey with the tights and you're dressed for winter.

Short sleeved jerseys are best suited for hotter conditions. Most jerseys feature three pockets at the rear for storage and some even come with zipped closures for improved security. The cycling jersey plays an important part in the overall layering which we cover later.

A lightweight short sleeve jersey is ideal as a base layer or worn on its own in summer.

A good long sleeve jersey keeps you warm in the cold and wicks sweat away from your body when the going gets tough.

Baggy shorts often feature a tight fitting Lycra or cotton inner short to give good support and padding.

MTB specific 'baggies' are loose fitting and more casual looking but don't skimp on performance.

Women's needs

Because most mountain bikers are male, very little is made of the fact that women riders can often benefit from specifically designed clothes, bikes and componentry.

It may seem an obvious statement, but women's physiques differ from men's. Typically women have shorter arms, shorter torsos, longer legs and a higher hip swivel point than their male counterparts. This has a big effect on bike design. Until recently women had to make do with a bike geometry that was designed around the male physique. Feminine adaptations were few and far between and typically comprised token efforts assigned to hybrid and shopper bikes.

Ladies' specific clothing is tough and technical, and is often designed to be worn for a variety of sports or gym sessions.

A long sleeve jersey is contoured to fit in all the right places.

Lycra shorts are shaped differently to men's and feature a specially shaped chamois insert to maximise comfort.

Full length or 'three-quarter' leggings offer increased warmth and protection and are therefore popular winter apparel.

Fortunately, as the sport has become more popular things have changed and manufacturers have realised there's money to be made in women specific bikes and componentry. These days every major bike brand has its own range of women-specific mountain bikes. They're serious bikes and the range of products caters for the amateur enthusiast right up to competitive racer.

The main difference between the standard, male orientated mountain bike and the women-specific model is the frame geometry. This usually comprises a shorter top tube and stem to account for shorter arms and torso, creating a better balanced riding position and increasing control over the front end.

Fitting women-specific componentry will further improve comfort. One of the best comfort enhancers is a women's saddle. These are shorter in the nose and wider at the rear to offer more support. Some will feature a hollowed area in the nose, providing a softer area for more delicate regions. Such saddles are so comfy that the concept's been incorporated into male saddle design and is now commonplace on many saddles.

Brake levers for women often come with a shorter reach to account for smaller hands and this even extends to the grips, which often have a reduced diameter.

Some manufacturers even equip specific tyres that are slightly wider, or softer treaded, the thinking being

that a softer tyre feel will offer greater cushioning to the rider. The assumption, possibly misguided, is that women riders value comfort more than men.

All this gender-specific componentry is now available in regular bike shops so converting an ordinary mountain bike into a more female orientated one should be a fairly simple exercise. Often swapping the saddle, fitting a shorter stem and adding a riser bar is all that's really needed. Other little touches, like increasing the tyre width to improve comfort and adding twist shifters, which are easier to operate than thumb shifters if you have small hands, can also make a big difference.

Feminine touches don't stop at the bike. Women specific ride clothing is also improving and, although not yet entirely commonplace, it's getting an increasing amount of floor space in bike shops. Fortunately what's on the shelves is of high quality.

The most important women-specific garments are shorts. As with bikes the women's versions vary from the men's. A different cut and specially shaped insert works better with the female form. The winning comfort combination is a women's saddle and shorts. The rest of the clothing is similar to male options. The same high-tech materials are used, while cut and colour schemes vary slightly. Lots of the clothes are designed to be suitable for cross training too, offering great value for money.

A women's specific saddle and shorts is a winning combination for comfort.

Seasonal layering

Many riders, especially beginners, shun the principles of layering that have been so heavily publicised in the outdoor leisure clothing industry. In mountain biking, layering is more important than ever. Three thin layers is always better than two thick ones, and we now have a great choice of under, over and in between garments to choose from.

Clothing is our second skin and the only protection we have against the elements. However, many riders often overlook the need for appropriate clothing and make do rather than taking time to think about how their clothes work in different conditions. One minute you'll be sweating on a long climb, the next you'll be chilled to the bone on a gusty descent.

The key to being properly dressed is to build up a good lightweight layering system that's breathable and works with your body to adapt to changing conditions. How you build up a layering system largely depends on the weather and the way it's likely to change. In hotter weather you need lightweight breathable clothing that's comfortable in the warm but capable of coping with the cold and wet should things turn nasty. As seasons turn colder and wetter, warmth and protection becomes the dominant factor.

Start with a base layer, whatever the weather. Technical materials in summer vests wick away the moisture in summer. Tour de France riders wear what look like string vests under their race jerseys, even on the sweltering climbs. They wear these to move moisture quickly away from the body to the jersey where it can evaporate to keep the body cool and dry. The vest then adds a bit of warmth for the fast descent.

In winter the base layer consists of a long sleeved thermal made from a technical fabric that's designed not only to wick moisture away from the body but also keep you warm. The filaments of the base layers are specifically designed to move sweat outwards by capillary action but they also trap a layer of warm air next to the skin.

Next comes the mid layer. This broad category comprises anything you might wear over a base layer and under an outer jacket. In summer a mid layer is probably the outer layer. It'll be loose-fitting and airy, basically a jersey designed to keep you as cool as possible.

A long sleeved jersey is more appropriate in winter. Even a light, snug-fitting fleece might be worth considering if it's really cold. Some jerseys feature a lightly brushed fabric for extra warmth, while others incorporate windproof fronts for improved wind protection. So your mid layer can be anything from a light fleece to a long sleeved jersey. The weather conditions will always dictate what you wear but the trick is to go for an all-purpose mid layer to get maximum use.

The final layer of protection comes from the outer shell. Think light and breathable, and the smaller the pack size the better, as most of the time you'll be carrying the top rather than wearing it. A shower-proof jacket should see you through most of the summer and milder spring/autumn conditions. Windproof and breathable are the all-important components. Even if you're wet you'll remain warm if you can stop the windchill.

When the cold creeps in, your outer layer needs to get heavier duty. The typical lightweight waterproof and breathable jackets (possibly over-trousers too) will be made from a high performance material that shuns water but allows sweat to escape. The heavier duty solutions are the ultimate in foul weather protection.

Summer

A short sleeve top and shorts will keep you cool and comfortable and can be worn as a base layer under warmer togs too.

Spring/autumn

A long sleeve mid layer and long tights are essential for warmth and protection when the temperatures drop.

Winter

Lightweight, waterproof and breathable, an outer shell and over-trousers will keep you dry and prevent windchill.

Weather proofing

Protecting yourself from the elements owes much to sensible clothing, but sensible component choices, like Crudguards and fork boots, should not be overlooked. Waterproof outer layers, water-resistant socks, even proofed tights and neckwear, are only part of the solution.

Ear warmers keep out biting chills.

Winter gloves will help you keep a grip on the bars in all weathers.

Waterproof socks improve comfort in the wet.

There's no need to hang up your bike and go into hibernation as the bad weather moves in. Weather proofing of both your clothing and your bike will see you through the worst of conditions.

As we've already mentioned, the last line of defence against the elements is the outer shell. This consists of a windproof, waterproof, breathable jacket, even over-trousers if the conditions are really bad. Proper riding jackets are designed with long backs to keep you covered when you're in the saddle.

If you wear a helmet there's no real need for a hood on a bike jacket but pockets are useful, especially if you carry a map. You'll notice that the cycling-specific outer shells hug the body more than jackets designed for walkers. This decreases wind resistance and bulk and reduces the snagging potential, but don't go for a jacket that's so tight it restricts your movement.

Arm and leg warmers are a quick and convenient way to add a bit of extra winter warmth with minimum fuss. Full-length thermal tights keep your legs warm and protected, and some even come with a lining of wind or waterproof fabric for extra protection against wheel spray.

Head and ear warmers protect the extremities from biting chills and a thick pair of winter specific riding gloves will take care of the hands. Thin tube-scarves (like the ones from Buff) fill draught gaps around the neck and they can also double up as ear and head warmers.

Neoprene overshoes warm the feet and protect against spray and you can further improve comfort with a pair of winter specific shoes or waterproof socks.

There are numerous products you can buy to protect the bike from the elements. Mudguards are obvious add-ons. Crud Catchers/Crud Guards are an MTB market leader. They fit to the down tube of the frame and to the rear seatpost. Their light weight and robust design makes them the perfect choice for the mountain bike.

Lizard Skins make various neoprene covers that are designed to protect the vulnerable parts of the bike, such as the headset and rear shock. These are great for protecting componentry but it's important to take them off from time to time, ideally when cleaning, as they can also hold dirt and grime in place.

Cables, especially the ones for the gears, are prone to contamination from dirt. Regular cleaning after muddy rides will ensure their smooth running. Sealed cables are designed to keep on running in bad conditions but have the disadvantage of being expensive and tricky to install.

Tyre choice is also important. Swapping to a set of winter tyres with more aggressive tread patterns will increase traction in the mud. While it may initially seem that bigger treaded tyres might be best in winter, the reality of the situation is that the best muddy condition tyres are thinner to increase mud clearance between the tyre and frame. They'll usually feature widely spaced tread patterns to allow mud to be shed more easily.

Remember, prevention is always better than cure. The best way to keep a bike running smoothly through poor trail conditions is through regular cleaning and maintenance.

Shoes and helmets

The trend towards casual wear doesn't stop at shorts and jerseys. Shoe and helmet designs follow suit and are also designed to offer the same high level of technical performance while improving the overall look.

Shoes

The shoes designed to be used with clipless pedals fall into two main categories: the race shoe and the trail shoe. The trail shoe looks more like a beefed up trainer and is designed to be softer and easier to walk in compared to the rigid race shoe. It features a stiff mid section for efficient power transfer but has more forgiving front and rear sections to improve walking comfort. It's extremely comfy and casual looking but is also designed to withstand the rigours of the trail.

Race shoes are all about power transfer. You can still walk in them but they're designed to be as inflexible as possible to provide the best power transfer to the pedals. The midsoles are rigid along the entire length and are usually made from toughened plastic or, on the more costly offerings, carbon fibre. Velcro straps and buckles replace laces for tight fit, and studs at the toe increase grip for sprinting up climbs. Like the trail shoes they're tough, but are better suited to full time pedalling than walking. The general rule of thumb is that trail shoes go with baggy shorts and race shoes go with Lycra.

Helmets

Helmets vary enormously in design and price. When choosing a helmet always go for one that fits properly rather than being swayed by an ill-fitting one you like the look of. Everyone's head is different so try on as many different designs as possible as shapes and fit differ between manufacturers.

Helmets are constructed from an interior of expanded polystyrene (EPS) and incorporate an outer shell to protect the helmet from day-to-day knocks. The EPS core is designed to absorb the impact energy of a crash. One big hit and a helmet is designed to break up in a controlled manner. They're only designed to work once and even if you can't see any damage you should replace your helmet after a spill.

A lot of research and development goes into the design of helmets. This is reflected in the price. In general, the greater number of vents the more work has gone into making the structure strong, the higher the cost and the more stylish the helmet. The vents are important. They're designed to let air circulate and cool the head, particularly important in hot climates.

Peaks are another feature to look out for, and they're more than just a cosmetic afterthought. They keep sun and rain out of your eyes, help to deflect low lying branches and will snap off in the event of a crash.

Trail shoes are particularly popular with beginners as they are comfy, casual looking and designed to work with clipless pedals as well as flat 'platform' ones.

Race shoes offer high performance when clipped in but are better suited to pedalling than walking.

A well-vented helmet is usually a sign of quality and performance. A peak at the front keeps rain and sun out of your eyes.

Helmets come in all manner of shapes, sizes and designs. Most manufacturers do kid-specific lids too.

Trailside repair kit

Every rider should have a compact trailside repair kit, easy to carry on or off the bike and with the necessary kit for emergencies. It's important to carry a compact repair kit to deal with any unforeseen mechanical problems when out on the trail. This doesn't mean packing the whole tool kit. The idea is to go light and carry the bare minimum of tools.

The most common problem that you should always be prepared for is a puncture. As a rule, these are easily fixed with very little stress or mechanical know-how. It's a lot quicker to carry a spare tube than mess around with glue and patches out on the trail. However, it's still worth carrying a repair kit, or glueless patches, especially on long rides – there's no telling how many punctures you'll experience, and if you run out of tubes you'll have to fix the holed tubes.

Inner tubes are no good without a pump. Mini pumps are specifically designed to be small and light. Most come with clips that enable them to be fitted to the frame, convenient for carrying them at all times.

A good multi-tool usually has everything you need for make-do repairs. They come in various shapes, sizes and prices. All should feature a set of Allen keys, which are essential for tightening most components on the bike, along with a Phillips and a flat nosed screwdriver.

A chain tool, for splitting, joining or removing damaged links from the chain, is another must. If the multi-tool doesn't feature one then you can buy one separately.

A spoke key is useful for straightening a buckled wheel, but if you're not particularly mechanically minded they can be more trouble than they're worth.

As well as the obligatory pump, tube and multi-tool there are a few other small things that, although not necessary, can come in useful. Binding tape, or electrician's insulating tape, has a multitude of uses, from a temporary bandage to mending a torn tyre. There's no need to take out the whole roll, cut off a length and wrap it around your pump. Zip ties and toe straps are also worth packing. And an energy bar hidden away will see you through those wobbly-knee moments.

If you're venturing into remote areas you need to expand your survival kit. Always take water, a map and a compass, or even a GPS receiver if you're feeling flash or your adventure is going to be truly exotic. A first-aid kit is always invaluable and consider packing a survival bag or space blanket (survival bags are better as you can get inside them).

The merits of mobile phones are obvious but many can't pick up a signal in the hills. Riding in groups and informing people of your planned route is the best way of remaining safe.

Use a saddlebag or backpack to carry your supplies. Backpacks are the most versatile because of their size and they also keep everything out of the dirt. Avoid cumbersome saddlebags as they can get in the way and kit tends to rattle around inside.

Stash your trail repair kit in a handy saddle pack. Always carry a mini pump.

CHAPTER 8

Technique and skills

It's said that once you've learnt how to ride a bike, you never forget. But simply riding a bike and riding a mountain bike on tough terrain are two very different things. This chapter will take you through the MTB skills learning curve, from the crucial but often misunderstood process of setting up your bike properly to tackling the ups, downs, twists and turns of technically challenging terrain at speed.

Bike set-up

Fine-tuning your bike's set-up so that it fits you properly means you'll get the most out of your riding. You can adjust the position of the saddle, handlebars, gear and brake controls to achieve the best balance of comfort and control in all situations – and avoid numb backsides and stiff backs. All it takes is a few minutes with some basic tools – a set of Allen keys is all that's normally needed.

Top tip

There's always the exception that proves the rule, and in mountain biking there are many occasions when a lower saddle is a better bet. Downhillers, slalom racers and dirt jumpers usually run low saddles for greater manoeuvrability and to keep their centre of gravity low. For any situation that involves extended periods of pedalling, it's better to put the saddle at the 'right' height. But for particularly steep descents or tricky trail obstacles, there's nothing wrong with lowering the saddle and getting it out of harm's way.

Setting the correct saddle height will improve your pedalling efficiency and keep your joints spinning smoothly.

Getting the saddle height right is important for efficient pedalling and healthy joints. Sit on the saddle and put a heel on one of the pedals with the crank at the bottom of its stroke. It helps to have a wall to lean against, or a friend to hold you upright. Now raise or lower the seatpost until your leg is completely extended. With your feet in their normal pedalling position your legs should now have a very slight bend at the knee when the cranks are at the bottom of their stroke. Too high and your hips will rock as you pedal; too low and you'll be straining your knee joints and leg muscles unnecessarily.

New riders often feel most comfortable with an upright riding position because it feels more like walking, and it's easy to look around at the view. But most bikes designed for all-round use have the handlebars an inch or two lower than the level of the saddle to allow some of the rider's weight to be supported by their arms. This helps position the combined centre of gravity of bike and rider between the front and rear wheels and improves control in tricky situations.

Most bikes have a stack of washers underneath the stem to allow fine tuning of handlebar height, while the distance between saddle and handlebars can also be tweaked by moving the saddle backwards and forwards on its rails. As a rule, aim for a 90 degree angle between torso and arms when sitting on the bike. If your bike is the right size for you, there's a good chance that the stock stem will give a good riding position. However, if you have unusually long or short arms or torso – women, for example, generally have short torsos relative to their leg length – you may find that a longer or shorter stem is more comfortable.

Taking control

Gear and brake levers should be set up so that they're within comfortable reach in all situations. Levers that are set too high put a great deal of stress on the tendons and muscles in your wrists, while if they're too low they can be dangerously hard to reach quickly.

Rotating grip-type shifters don't need much in the way of adjustment, although they can be twisted round the bar so that the gear display window is easy to see. Separate underbar trigger-type shifters should be rotated so that they're comfortably within reach. An angle of 45 degrees for the brake levers is about right – you should be able to extend your fingers and reach the lever blades without rotating your wrists away from your normal riding position.

Brake lever reach can be adjusted for smaller hands by using the grub screw on the clamp body, which brings the lever closer towards the handlebars. You may also need to adjust the brake pads and/or cable – if in doubt, consult your dealer.

To tilt or not to tilt?

The saddle should be set as close to level as possible. Raising the nose can cause obvious problems with pain in the pelvic region, but a low nose can be just as problematic by putting unnecessary stress on arms, wrists and back. Slackening the saddle clamp bolt on the seat post head allows adjustments to be made to the angle. Put a straight edge – like a ruler – across the top of your saddle to make sure it's level.

Brake levers should be set at an angle of approx 45 degrees. Riders with small hands may need to bring the levers more inboard so they can reach them quickly and easily.

Attack!

There's one essential technique every mountain biker needs to perfect: body language. The way you position yourself over the bike helps to determine how well you and your bike will cope with a wide variety of trail situations. Learning to use the 'attack' position is a key building block in becoming a better rider, opening up the door to many more advanced techniques. Good riders use the attack position automatically, without thinking, in any number of trail situations.

The idea is to be ready for anything the trail might throw at you, whether it's a sharp corner, an unexpected drop or a quick hop over a log.

Principal points

- **Knees bent** *To absorb trail impacts and to allow weight shifts over the bike.*
- **Elbows bent** *Makes it easy to lift the front wheel and helps to absorb trail vibrations.*
- **Bum above the saddle** *Allows the bike to move around and makes it easy to shift weight forwards or backwards.*
- **Pedals level** *Keeps your weight centred over the bike, maintains maximum obstacle clearance and allows for sudden pedalling bursts.*
- **Look ahead** *Plan your line choice in advance and keep an eye out for trail obstacles.*
- **Brakes covered** *In situations where it may be necessary to slow down fast.*
- **Relax!** *The key to the attack position.*

To use the attack position raise yourself slightly off the saddle, bending your knees with the pedals roughly level to absorb trail shocks. Keeping your back flat, bend your elbows and stay relaxed, allowing the bike to move around underneath you but keeping a firm grip on the bars in order to be able to respond to the trail quickly. Your weight should be centred between the front and rear wheels, giving the maximum possible traction and control in any situation. Staying relaxed is the key to the attack position's effectiveness, and tensing up is the most common mistake. Remember: bent knees, bent elbows, let the bike float beneath you.

It's a good idea to cover the brake levers with a couple of fingers in case you need to scrub off speed quickly, but on particularly smooth surfaces – or where you can see a long way ahead – it may not be essential. In any case, keep looking well ahead, picking your line as you go and watching for unexpected obstacles. Don't look at the front wheel, and never look at an obstacle you want to avoid – pick a line around it instead. It's a golden rule of mountain biking that the bike will run into any obstacle that you stare at long enough, so, however tempting it may be to keep an eye on that errant rock/root/ditch…don't. Force yourself to look at where you want to go, and the bike will follow. Experienced riders read the trail ahead by scanning continuously between two points – well ahead of the bike to check for changes in trail direction, stray walkers or obvious obstacles, and a few yards ahead of the front wheel to double-check that the bike's still on a safe line.

Practise the attack position on an easy, level trail and get used to the feeling of the bike moving around beneath you. While you should be relaxed, you also need to feel in control of the bike. It should be possible to shift quickly between sitting, the attack position and any number of variants – cornering, speed jumping, descending, and so on – quickly and smoothly. Whenever the speed picks up, the trail gets bumpy or you're uncertain what's around the next corner, go into attack mode and you'll be ready for anything.

Common mistakes

Although front and rear suspension make life easier, most mountain bike techniques are best tackled with the rider's weight lifted slightly above the saddle. Beginners have a tendency to stay seated as long as possible, reducing the bike's ability to float over obstacles and adding greatly to any potential discomfort.

The other common mistake is to tense up. Even experienced riders often have to consciously remind themselves to relax. The attack position allows you – the rider – to stay in control of the bike in almost any situation. Thinking yourself into a relaxed state of mind while your bike's bucking around underneath you is a counter-intuitive but essential technique.

Building blocks

The attack position is the basis for the vast majority of mountain bike skills – any riding technique, in fact, that doesn't involve sitting on the saddle:

- Cornering
- Descending
- Drop-offs
- Front wheel lofts
- Speed jumps
- Bunny hops
- Standing climbing

It's probably the most versatile technique you'll ever learn – well worth perfecting.

Keeping your knees and elbows bent enables you to stay relaxed, absorb trail bumps and shift your weight around over the bike. Keep your eyes on the trail ahead (left).

Stop

The principle of a brake is simple. The rotating motion of a wheel is converted to heat by the friction generated between pad and braking surface – either the rim or a separate disc. The faster the conversion of forward motion to heat energy, the quicker the bike slows down. On a mountain bike there's a further limiting factor – the available grip between tyre and ground. Once the coefficient of friction between the two is exceeded, the tyre slides over the ground and the brake's effectiveness is severely diminished. Or, to put it another way, skidding isn't a good way to scrub off speed...

Top tip

Try adjusting your brakes so that pads contact about halfway through the lever's travel – it doesn't affect power, and can reduce hand fatigue on long descents.

V style rim brakes are cheap, lightweight and easy to maintain, the ideal braking system for anyone new to mountain biking. They're also pretty much standard spec on most bikes up to £800.

To avoid locking up wheels you need to squeeze – rather than pull – the brake levers. Try to get into the habit of riding with two fingers covering each brake lever at all times, so that you're ready to react to trail conditions and obstacles. Develop a feel for what's happening beneath the bike and learn to read the trail surface, adjusting speed and the degree to which the brakes are used to suit the conditions. On long descents, for example, it's easier and safer to maintain a constant speed by 'feathering' the brakes – squeezing them gently as needed – than to grab handfuls at intervals.

There's also the issue of weight distribution. Forget what you were taught when you first learnt to ride a bike – the front brake is your best friend, and the faster you need to slow down, the more you need it. As you brake, rise out of the saddle and shift your weight rearwards to counteract the inevitable tendency to be thrown forward. The combined weight of your body and bike will tend to pivot forwards anyway, increasing traction at the front wheel and helping the whole process along. Just don't grab too big a handful of front brake.

Finally, remember that effective braking isn't just safer – it means you can ride faster, too. By braking as little, as late and as efficiently as possible you'll maintain your hard-won momentum, cover the ground faster and have more fun in the process.

Skids are for kids – and corners

There's always the exception that proves the rule, and there are times when a controlled skid can be useful. In most circumstances the drastically reduced braking effectiveness and potential for ripping up the trail mean that locked up wheels should be avoided, but in certain cornering situations a controlled rear wheel slide can be helpful.

On very tight corners – a downhill singletrack switchback, for example – sliding the back wheel round is sometimes the only effective way to avoid a dismount. More often a rear wheel drift is used as a fast cornering technique in downhill racing. In both cases the principle is the same – the rear brake is pulled on hard and the rider's weight used to flick the back end of the bike round, forcing the rear wheel into a controlled slide. The brake is released when the bike is pointing in the right direction.

It goes without saying that it's a tricky technique to do well, and it's only advisable on trail surfaces that'll withstand the extra wear and tear – gravel or hardpacked tracks, for example.

What brake – disc or rim?

Bicycles have been using rim brakes for decades. The advantages of a rim brake are simplicity, low weight and price, and easy maintenance. The disadvantages include reduced effectiveness in wet conditions, wear and tear on the rim and the need for the braking surface of the rim to run flat and true.

Disc brakes have been around for a long time too, but their use on mountain bikes is relatively new. They're far less affected by wet or muddy conditions than rim brakes and don't rely on the truth of the wheel, so they're a good choice for downhill racing – although they're becoming increasingly popular for recreational and trail riding, too.

The best – and most expensive – disc brakes use hydraulic fluid to operate the caliper. Cheaper cable operated brakes should theoretically offer similar levels of stopping power, but early attempts have suffered from being designed down to a price. We're only just beginning to see the first of a new generation of well designed, affordable and powerful cable disc brakes.

For increased braking power and better performance in the wet and slime try disc brakes. There are two disc options: hydraulic or cable operated.

Going down

Everyone likes riding downhill – it's fast, fun, and involves relatively little effort. The key to faster, safer, smoother descending is simple – control. Because riding downhill involves higher speeds than you'll otherwise encounter, it's absolutely essential to be able to react quickly to a rapidly changing situation.

Top tip

- On very steep sections or in any situation where you're feeling uncertain, drop your saddle – it makes it easier to get your weight right back, and makes unexpected and unscheduled dismounts less painful. A quick release on the seatpost makes this job quick and simple.

- Descents tend to bounce the chain around. To minimise rattling shift the chain onto the big chainring and one of the three or four largest sprockets at the rear. This increases the spring tension in the rear mech and helps keep the chain where it's supposed to be.

- On fast or very bumpy descents, hitting an obstacle at speed with an under-inflated tyre can pinch the inner tube between rim and obstacle, splitting it and resulting in a 'pinch flat' with a sudden loss of air pressure. If in doubt, a little more tyre pressure goes a long way.

The starting point is the attack position. With elbows and knees bent, brakes covered and weight centred over the bike – or shifted slightly back, depending on the severity of the gradient – the bike will be able to float over small trail obstacles and you'll be in a position to respond to anything unexpected, like a corner or a particularly bumpy section of trail. Stay relaxed and consciously resist the temptation to tense up – a tense body is less able to respond to changes in the trail and more likely to sustain injuries if you do fall off.

Look well ahead and pick your preferred line in advance. The further down the trail you look, the faster you can safely go. Scan ahead as far as possible, glancing at the few yards ahead of your front wheel from time to time to look for unexpected obstacles. The bike will generally follow the line that you're concentrating on, so staring at the tree stump or rock that you want to avoid is a sure-fire recipe for a close encounter with the local flora. Above all, resist the temptation to concentrate on the trail just in front of you. Spotting obstacles and potential problems in plenty of time gives you all the leeway you need to brake, steer or pedal your way out of trouble before you get there.

Controlling your speed is all about predicting what's likely to happen in the next few seconds. Feather the brakes, squeezing the levers gently to control your speed according to the trail conditions and how far ahead you're able to see. On good surfaces with a clear view ahead of you it's safe to lay off the brakes and let gravity do its worst. On

steeper slopes, in situations where traction is limited or on a trail where the line ahead is obscured, you'll need to slow down. In any situation, plan ahead and avoid sudden braking.

When the going gets steep

Very steep or technical trails demand a slightly different approach. As the gradient increases, shift your weight back behind the saddle to keep your centre of gravity low and centred between the tyres. The steeper the slope, the further back your weight needs to be. In extreme situations it may be necessary to ride with the saddle against your chest, your arms fully extended and your weight right back over the rear tyre. Feather the brakes carefully to control your speed. The front brake is far more effective than the rear in this situation, but be prepared to back off if the front wheel starts to slide.

Drop-offs

Drop-offs mark a sudden drop in the trail from one level to another – a step, for example. Depending on the height of the drop, the simplest approach is often to shift your weight back, drop the front wheel over and let the rear follow through. A quicker technique for small to medium sized drops is to pull a small wheelie off the lip and land both wheels at the same time. As the front wheel approaches the lip, push down on the bars and immediately pull back up. At lower speeds it helps to add a half pedal stroke at the same time. As the bike drops off, be prepared to absorb the landing by bending your arms and legs.

Lowering your saddle before tackling a steep descent will enable you to shift your weight to the back of the bike.

Practise lifting up the front wheel before a drop-off, it's a faster and smoother trail technique than simply rolling off it.

Going up

Nobody likes climbing, but there are a few techniques that can help get you uphill faster and with less effort. First, accept that it's going to be uncomfortable. Knowing that it's going to hurt means that when it does, it won't be such an unpleasant surprise. Second, think in terms of riding over – rather than up – the hill. Mentally preparing yourself for riding over the summit means you can carry on riding without collapsing at the top in a hyper-ventilating heap.

Top tip

Check your tyre pressures, particularly at the rear. On climbs where traction is at a premium, letting a few pounds of pressure out of the rear tyre can sometimes make the difference between riding and walking to the top.

Going up requires a different riding position than descending. As the gradient increases shift your weight forward to stop the front wheel lifting off the ground.

By far the most common mistake is to start out too fast. Your body takes a while to adapt to the increased cardiovascular load imposed by climbing, so on long climbs, start out slowly so that you can pace yourself. A few minutes into the climb your heart rate and breathing should have settled into a steady pattern.

The effort should be noticeable, but you should feel as though you have some energy in reserve. Match your breathing to your pedal strokes, picking a gear that allows you to turn the pedals smoothly and easily. As the gradient increases flatten your back, drop your wrists and shift forward on the saddle to help keep the front wheel from lifting. Concentrate on your breathing, keeping it smooth, steady and regular. Turn the pedals in smooth circles, picking your gear in advance so that you don't have to shift under pressure. And keep your upper body as still as possible – rocking from side to side simply wastes valuable energy.

Climbing out of the saddle is a useful technique in two situations. Firstly, it can help to rest hard-working muscle groups on a long climb. Second, it can be used to maximise power output. Shift into a slightly harder gear – a couple of clicks at the rear is usually about right – and stand up with your arms slightly bent at the elbows. On short sections which need added grunt, use the extra leverage of this position to convert your body weight into forward motion via the pedals. Remember to keep your weight back to keep the rear wheel gripping, and plan ahead so that you can downshift and sit back down again before too long – standing climbing is extremely tiring.

Climbing walls

As a climb steepens you need to adjust your riding position to compensate. Shift your weight forwards on the saddle and drop your upper body by bending your arms. Flattening your wrists and pulling back, rather than up, on the bars also reduces the natural tendency of the front wheel to lift as the gradient increases. Keeping your weight low, shift your weight backwards and forwards on the saddle to maintain grip at the rear.

Technical climbs

Technical climbs add tricky obstacles to the equation, scattering anything from loose gravel and rocks to roots, ledges and sudden gradient changes in your path. Coping with these extra demands on balance and coordination while your body's already under huge aerobic stress is difficult, but not necessarily impossible.

The key is to plan ahead. Pick your line and gear in advance, shifting early so that you don't have to change gear under load. Shift your weight forwards and backwards – even the smallest, subtlest movement can make a difference – to balance the conflicting demands of keeping the front wheel planted on terra firma and the rear wheel turning. Keeping your upper body low, your wrists bent downwards and your bum shifted forwards on the saddle will all help in steep, loose, marginal situations.

Ride smart, breathe right

Most of the time you'll be climbing aerobically, using oxygen to help break down glycogen fuel stored in your body and convert it into usable energy for your muscles. This is the most efficient way to ride, although it only works at a steady pace. For short bursts needing more speed or power – perhaps a steep section on a climb – the body switches to anaerobic mode, completing the energy conversion without the help of oxygen. This is a very inefficient way to ride, and is only sustainable over short distances. For any climb lasting more than 20 seconds or so, aim to take things steady and use your body's aerobic system. You'll get there quicker and with less effort.

Look well ahead and choose your line, that way you can assess the trail surface and make the right gear selections in plenty of time.

For any climb lasting more than 20 seconds aim to take things steady to keep the flow of oxygen to your muscles.

The bends

Cornering

Cornering on a bike isn't quite as straightforward as it first appears. Everyone thinks that they corner by turning the handlebars – but in fact there's a whole lot more going on. As the speed increases, turning the bars becomes a lot less important than braking, line choice and weight distribution. Two tricks in particular will help you tackle corners faster, smoother and in greater control. The first is to make the corner bigger than it actually is. Racing drivers use this technique all the time, approaching wide, cutting close to the apex and exiting wide. The effect is to increase the bend's radius, allowing a faster approach and exit speed. The second is to use your weight to increase the tyre's grip. This is a technique which works in all but the slowest, sharpest turns. It relies on resting all your weight on the outside pedal – the left pedal for a right-hand bend, for example – and avoiding putting any pressure on the inside pedal. By doing this you're forcing your centre of gravity closer to the tyre's contact patch with the ground as the bike leans, increasing their traction in the process. It also has the benefit of raising the inside pedal out of harm's way and increasing ground clearance.

Top tip

A suspension fork can help keep the front wheel firmly planted over trail obstacles, improving grip and increasing speed through the corners. Skilled riders shift their weight forwards slightly in the corners to make the fork work harder and maximise front tyre traction – but it's a technique to be used with caution. A sliding front tyre is very hard to recover, whereas a rear-wheel skid needn't be disastrous.

Preparation is the key to better cornering. As you approach a bend get ready by using the attack position, assessing how far ahead you can see and how fast you can safely ride the corner. Remember that there might be other trail users just out of sight, so err on the side of caution. Scrub off your speed in plenty of time as you approach, so as to avoid braking once you're turning – a braking bike is far harder to control in a turn. Lean the bike into the bend, but keep your body upright and rest all your weight on the outside pedal.

Many riders make the mistake of leaning both bike and body or keeping their pedals level, both of which decrease the tyre's ability to grip in the turn. Where there's space, cut in to the apex of the corner and exit wide. Cover both brakes in case you need to adjust your speed further, and look well ahead. As soon as you can see the trail straighten out it's safe to straighten up, get back on the power and build your speed up again.

Singletrack

Sections of singletrack provide one of the most satisfying mountain bike experiences, placing great demands on a rider's skill. Tight, bike-width trails often twist and turn, combining sudden changes in height and direction with a variety of surfaces. In situations where the trail is too narrow to choose a line or is littered with obstacles, standard cornering techniques – dropping the outside pedal, for example, or using the apex to increase its radius – can be tricky. Maintaining momentum is the key, planning ahead to minimise sudden changes in speed so that one corner flows smoothly and easily into the next. If pedal clearance is an issue – in wooded singletrack, for example, or in rocky areas – it may be safer to ride the corners in the attack position with both pedals level, slowing down a little to compensate. Keep looking well down the trail, using the brakes sparingly and riding at a speed that allows you to comfortably stay in control.

Tight turns

Very tight corners depend on low-speed balance and coordination. As with fast cornering, approach in the attack position and slow down in plenty of time. Keep the brakes covered and your weight out of the saddle, turning the bars into the corner with your pedals level and the bike upright or tilted very slightly into the bend. Allow the bike to roll slowly through the corner, dragging the rear brake if necessary. Avoid using the front brake – it will tend to tuck the front wheel more tightly into the turn. Straighten up as you exit the turn, bearing in mind that the rear wheel will take a tighter line to the front and may need to be coaxed over obstacles on the inside of the corner.

A good pair of suspension forks will improve your grip and speed through corners.

When the trail is narrow keep looking well ahead so you're ready for any twists, turns or obstacles that the trail will throw up.

In tight corners cover the brakes, keep your weight out of the saddle and tilt the bike slightly into the bend.

Clearing obstacles

Part of the challenge of riding off-road is handling anything the trail can throw at you. Switching from sitting down to standing in the attack position and letting the bike move around underneath you will cope with the vagaries of most trail surfaces, but occasionally you'll come across something bigger – a log, say, or a ditch – blocking your path. Unexpected obstacles like these needn't interrupt the rhythm of your ride once you know how to cope with them.

Top tip

Practise speed and bunny hops by using an obstacle that won't wreck you or your bike if you get things wrong – a stick balanced across a couple of stones should do the trick. Increase the approach speed and height of the obstacle as your confidence increases.

If you're not already a bunny-hop king, investing in a set of clipless pedals and shoes will help you lift the back end of the bike up more easily. Some say it's cheating, of course…

The simplest way to clear an obstacle without getting off and walking is to lift the front wheel over it. Provided it's not too large, a correctly timed hoist of the front wheel is usually enough – the back wheel will follow through of its own accord with a little forward momentum and a helping hand from the rider. Pulling up on the handlebar will lift the front, although for taller obstacles a half pedal stroke at the same time will give a little extra height. In effect, you're pulling a mini wheelie. Unweighting the rear by shifting your weight forward at the right moment will help it to follow the front wheel's lead, especially with larger obstacles. It's surprising just what you can ride over with this simple technique – practice, timing and confidence are the key to getting it right.

At speed, and with small to medium sized obstacles, lifting both wheels clear of the ground simultaneously – a speed hop – or in rapid succession – a bunny hop – means you can carry on riding without interrupting the flow. In effect these are both condensed and immaculately timed versions of the low-speed technique. As you approach in the attack position, crouch over the bike with your arms and legs bent and your wrists flat. At the last moment compress your arms and legs and spring upwards, rotating your wrists forward and lifting with both arms and legs to bring both wheels off the ground.

Clipless pedals are a big help in lifting the rear of the bike, although skilled riders can hoist the rear wheel several feet clear of the ground even with flat pedals. Absorb the landing by bending your arms and legs as the wheels hit the ground, and carry on riding.

Speed or bunny?
The speed hop and bunny hop are close cousins. The bunny hop involves lifting front and rear wheels separately – the front first, followed closely by the rear. It's harder to get the timing right, but it's more versatile than the speed hop because it means that obstacles can be cleared at a range of different speeds. The speed hop lifts both wheels simultaneously. It's easier to master, but relies entirely on the forward speed of the bike to clear both wheels over the obstacle.

Which pedal?
Skilled riders are capable of lifting the rear wheel with flat pedals. On the face of it this is a move that defies the laws of physics, but it's a technique widely employed by trials riders, downhill racers and dirt jumpers. Mere mortals usually find it easier to hoist the back of the bike with feet firmly attached to the pedals, which is where clipless pedals are useful. Unless you particularly need flat pedals for your type of riding, investing in a pair of clipless pedals – with shoes to match – will open up a new world of riding skills.

Chainring grinders
There's a practical limit to the size of obstacle you can safely ride over at low speeds. Once the front wheel is clear, there's a danger of fouling the large chainring before the rear wheel has a chance to follow through. In the case of logs, the chainring may simply dig in. On rocks, the risk of damaging the chainring – bending, chipping or breaking off a tooth, for example – is considerable. If in doubt, check before you attempt to ride over it. Above the chainring-grinding size is a larger class of obstacle that may, in some cases, still be ridable. If the front wheel is still in contact with the rock or log as the rear wheel reaches it, there's a good chance that the chainrings will clear – but obstacles this large need a good degree of commitment, skill and timing to ride over safely.

Even if you get your front wheel over a log, your chainring could easily come a cropper and you could end up losing a tooth, or worse.

CHAPTER 9

MTB
workshop

Looking after your bike is something you can do yourself, or you can take it to a shop and let a qualified mechanic do it. But even if you don't want to tackle the more complex stuff, it's worth getting to know the basics about what you should be looking out for in order to keep your bike running safely and efficiently. If you look after it properly it'll look after you.

Simple tools will allow you to carry out most bike maintenance jobs.

Wheel truing stands are useful, and don't have to be expensive.

The right tools

Home workshops: the basic collection & the luxury collection.

A typical collection of home workshop tools should include the following;

- Allen keys
- Chain tool
- Adjustable spanner
- Screwdrivers
- Pedal spanner
- Pliers
- Brush set for cleaning
- Bottom bracket tool
- Chain whip
- Grease
- Chain lube
- Cassette lockring removal tool
- Degreaser
- Spoke keys
- Cable cutters
- Cone spanners
- Chainring bolt spanner

Setting up a basic home workshop takes the hassle out of servicing your bike and will save you money in both the short and the long term. Bike mechanics isn't the dark art it sometimes appears to the uninitiated. It just needs practice and a bit of patience. The initial cost of tools soon pays for itself but best of all you become self-sufficient and learn how your bike works.

For most home fettlers all that's needed is a well stocked toolbox, but there's nothing to stop you going to town on a professional set-up. Whatever your ambitions technically there are a few basics that every home mechanic should carry.

Mini tools are adequate for the jobs out on the trail but you'll be better off with proper tools for the workshop. A quality set of ball ended

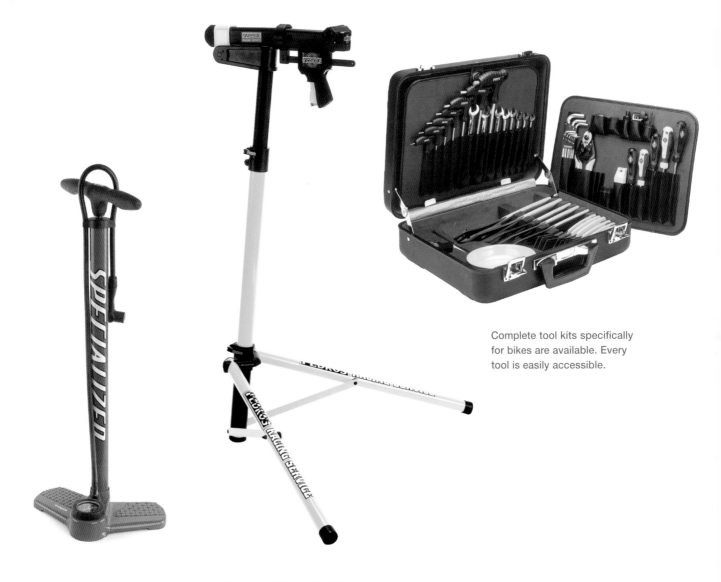

Complete tool kits specifically for bikes are available. Every tool is easily accessible.

A proper workshop track pump is a worthwhile aquisition.

If you want the perfect home workshop, treat yourself to a set-up like this, from US tool specialist Pedros.

Allen keys, sizes 1.5–10mm, is a good start. Bike specific cable cutters are designed to make light work of inner and outer cables and they do a much tidier job than electrical snips. Chains often need replacing so you'll need a chain tool, and tyre levers ease tube and tyre removal.

The drivetrain (gears) requires some specific tools. To remove the rear cassette you'll need a cassette lockring tool, chain whip and adjustable spanner. To reach the bottom bracket (BB) you'll need a crank extractor followed by a splined BB tool and an adjustable spanner to remove the BB. You'll need a spoke key for truing wheels and a set of cone spanners for servicing the hub bearings. Spoke nipples come in different sizes, so buy a multi-spoke key if you're not sure of the size.

Consumables like grease, chain lube, cables,

puncture patches and inner tubes are always handy items to have lying around. Washing fluids like citrus degreaser help when cleaning the bike and light oils such as WD-40 are useful for shifter units and cables.

Although not an essential, a good solid work stand makes life easier than bending over a bike perched against the kitchen table. The steady hand of a stand allows you tackle everything from a gear adjustment to a bottom bracket change with relative ease, and most are foldable for easy storage.

A good track pump is another labour saving device that will have you inflating tyres in seconds instead of struggling with a mini pump. High pressure shock pumps are essential if you run an air sprung fork/shock.

Cleaning

How to clean a mountain bike properly. Cleaning the bike needn't be the chore it appears. With the right kit and a bit of planning you can rattle through the process within a couple of minutes. Here's how…

Cleaning kit

Avoid the temptation to use a jetwash. The high pressured water can get between bearing surfaces and displace the grease. The light stream from a hose pipe is more suitable. A good brush will take the effort out of cleaning and will be perfect for getting into those hard to reach spots. Get some bike wash and degreaser and you're on your way.

Clean the frame

If you have any bike cleaner spray (this is usually a light degreaser) spray the whole frame with it. This will help to loosen the dirt. Give the cleaner some time to work (follow the instructions carefully as some degreasers will damage your graphics if you leave them on for too long) and then rinse the whole frame. It sometimes pays to go over the whole frame with a soapy sponge followed by another rinse if the bike is really dirty.

Special attention

Pay special attention to the suspension fork and rear shock. If the suspension fork comes with fork boots, lift them to allow any trapped water to escape. Wipe around the seals and stanchions with a rag and allow to dry. Do not use solvent-based sprays around fork and shocks. Only lubricate the stanchions with oils that have been recommended by the manufacturers.

Light shower

Start with the dirtiest jobs first. Use degreaser on the chain and gears to get them clean and a brush to get in between the sprockets of the cassette. Give the degreaser some time to work and then rinse the whole bike with low pressure water. Use a stout brush to get the mud off the tyres and rims.

Lubrication

Let the bike air dry (bounce it up and down to get rid of excess water) before applying fresh lube to the chain. This is when you should give the cables a clean but this will not be necessary after every wash. Working over the bike with a rag and a bit of light oil such as WD-40 will add a sheen to the frame and remove any streaks.

Disc brakes

Clean disc brakes with a specific cleaner. The pads and rotors of disc brakes hate grease. Even the oil from fingers affects their performance. If you're worried about contaminating the discs, remove the wheels from the bike and wash them separately.

Basic care and feeding

The essentials of lubrication. What to oil and grease.

The Chain

The chain comes in for a barrage of abuse and is often one of the most overlooked components. A quick clean after a dirty ride and a re-lube should keep it running smoothly.

The easiest way to clean the chain properly is to use a chain cleaner. You fill this device with degreaser and then fix it onto the chain. As you back pedal the chain is cleaned by the degreaser and a set of brushes housed inside. If you don't want to buy a chain cleaner, a cheaper way is to use an old toothbrush and some degreaser. Hold a pot under the chain so you can catch and reuse any spilt degreaser. After cleaning wash off the degreaser with water, allow the chain to dry and then re-lube.

At the same time as cleaning the chain, use a narrow brush to clean in between the sprockets on the cassette.

There are two types of chain lube: wet and dry. Wet lubes are the more traditional oils and are best suited to wet, muddy conditions. Dry lubes set dry and attract less dust but they're easily washed off. This makes them better suited to dry conditions. Apply lubes sparingly to each link and wipe away any excess.

Cables

Gear cables are a haven for dirt and grime. If not correctly looked after they'll soon clog up and cause the derailleurs to miss-shift. Again, the best way to look after cables is by regular cleaning. Little and often is the motto here. It's best to service the cables after cleaning the bike. Shift the chain into the lowest gear (biggest sprocket) at the rear and highest at the front (largest chainring). Now, without pedalling, release the cable tension by operating both shifters. This produces enough cable slack to remove the outers from the cable stops on the frame.

The same process can be carried out on brake cables. Release the brake at the wheel and then pull the outer cable from the frame's cable stops. Slide back the outers to expose the inner cable. Wipe the inner cables with a water-displacing oil like WD-40 or a light chain lube. Slide back the outers and replace them in the cable stops after cleaning.

It's important to keep things greased. The seat post is often overlooked but a light coating of grease will stop it binding in the frame. The same goes for the quick release wheel skewers. A thin layer of grease prevents them rusting and binding inside the hub axle.

Greasing of components like the headset, hubs, forks and rear shocks requires less frequent service intervals and a lot depends on how much you ride the bike. Servicing of these components is essential and is covered further on in this chapter.

A proper chain cleaning device is fairly cheap and a very useful way of extending your chain's life and keeping it running smooth.

Water and dirt get into cables by the frame stops. Remove outer cables from the stops occasionally and lubricate.

Problem spotting

Noises bikes make and how to solve them.

The silent, trouble-free bike is a bit of a Holy Grail when it comes to MTBs. There's nothing worse than riding along and having the constant irritation of a squeak, creak or rattle coming from somewhere on the bike. It's not always easy to locate the source of such noises, but once found they're usually easily cured.

Chain slap, where the chain bounces down onto the frame (and wrecks the paint) over bumpy terrain, is one of the loudest noises. Although it's hard to prevent (keep pedalling and avoid the bumps…) you can certainly reduce the noise and damage level. Fitting a protector strip, ideally a full wrap made from Neoprene, to the chainstay will help.

Rattles indicate that something is loose, worn out or ill-fitting. Check all nuts and bolts on the bike from time to time: chainrings, valve nuts, gear mechs, brake levers, calipers and blocks, saddles, pedals, etc. Even wheel quick releases can come loose if you haven't fastened them tight enough in the first place. Also check that peripheral items like saddlebags and frame mounted pumps are not rattling around. Finally, make sure all the major fixing bolts (bars, stems, seat posts, cranks) are tight.

Creaks when pedalling are one of the most common irritations, but they will often have nothing to do with the cranks and pedals. They may be simply deflected noise from your body movement on the bike elsewhere.

When tracing creaks, check that saddle bolts are tight and greased. A worn or slightly loose saddle can click like a worn bottom bracket and echo through the frame. Pedal while standing up to see if the noise stops. Once the saddle has been eliminated move to the cranks. Check for any play in the pedal bearings and make sure the bottom bracket cups, pedals and crank bolts are tight. Chainring bolts often work themselves loose. Make sure they are greased and done up tightly. Stainless steel chainring bolts are better than lightweight alloy ones as they can be done up tighter and they don't seize if greased.

The ear splitting sound of squealing brakes is the most irritating of all bike sounds. It lets people know you're coming, but a bell or a cough is so much more polite. There are times when brake screeching is simply a problem of incompatibility between rims and blocks, but you'll often find that removing the surface glaze from the rim and brake block with some wet and dry sandpaper goes a long way to stopping the noise. The same goes for disc brakes. Ensure the disc and pads are kept clean with a specific cleaner. Correctly setting up the rim brakes by toeing in the front end of the pad can also stop the noise.

Clunks emanating from the rear of a full suspension bike are often an indication of loose or worn bushings at the shock mounts. Knocking at the front could mean the fork bushings are worn or the headset is loose.

A Neoprene protection sheath is a great way of stopping your chain from damaging paintwork as it bounces around over the bumps.

Check tightness of crank bolts from time to time.

If your brakes are squealing, make sure the blocks are properly adjusted so that the front edge touches the rim first.

Wheel truing

How wheel building works and how you can true your own.

For the amateur mountain biker, it's not really necessary to know the finite ins and outs of wheel building. But it is helpful to know some basics so you can at least straighten a buckled wheel.

For general home maintenance you can get by without a special wheel jig. Most of the time all you are trying to do is remove the side-to-side imperfections in the wheel. First, remove the tyre and tube to reduce the forces on the rim. Make sure there is no play in the hub bearings.

Put the wheel back in the frame or fork then, using the brake blocks as a temporary guide, spin the wheel to find where the rim is out of line. This is where it touches the brake blocks. Concentrate on the larger imperfections and initially ignore the little ones.

The principle behind truing a wheel is to pull the rim back into line by tightening the spokes on the opposite side of the buckle and loosening those on the side of the buckle. Use a spoke key to turn the nipple. Spoke keys come in different gauges, but it's normally a choice between two. It is important to use the right size or you'll round the square edges of the spoke nipple. If you're unsure of the spoke nipple size get yourself a multi-key that will fit all the sizes.

As with most threads, clockwise tightens the spoke and anti-clockwise loosens it. Make small adjustments (a quarter to half a turn at a time) until the rim is pulled back in line. You will need to loosen the spokes opposite the ones you are tightening to even the tension and prevent the rim from being pulled down as well as to the side.

For the home mechanic removing the side wobbles is not difficult. If a wheel is damaged so much that it has major up and down deflections too, then it's usually time for a rebuild with a new rim and spokes.

Most tweaks can be done at home using the brake blocks as a temporary jig, but if you're serious about wheel building you'll need a proper jig. Professional level jigs can be expensive but there are many affordable ones on the market intended for the home mechanic.

The science and theory behind wheel building justifies a book in itself. The book that's widely regarded as a classic is *The Bicycle Wheel* by Jobst Brandt. There are also many websites on the subject.

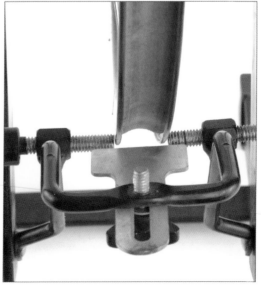

If you haven't got a wheel truing stand, remove the tyre and use tape between the fork legs to check for up and down distortions in the rim. Above: To find where side to side buckles are, hold your finger still and spin the wheel. The rim is straightened by tightening or loosening spokes, but take care... too much tightening/ loosening does more harm than good.
Left: Simple wheel truing devices are easier than the finger method.

Tyre care and puncture mending tips

Tread choices and pressures for different riders and terrain,

plus a brief run down on tyre care and puncture repair.

As with a race car, tyre selection can be crucial when it comes to the mountain bike. You won't need a quiver of tyres hung up in your house but there are a few pointers to ensure you get the most out of your rubber and match the right tyres to the conditions.

Tyres fall into two broad categories with most multi-condition models slotting in between. At the wet end of the scale the mud tyre is made for optimum grip in muddy conditions. It's thinner, to increase mud clearance between the tyre and frame, and features a more aggressive tread design than a dry weather tyre. The tread is also designed to shed mud rather than hold on to it. Mud tyres may be great for wet conditions but they're slow on hard dry ground due to the high rolling resistance of the tread knobbles.

Dry condition tyres are totally different. Mud clearance isn't a big issue so they can afford to be fatter. The bigger air volume adds comfort and the closely packed, low profile tread pattern reduces rolling resistance. Because dry condition tyres are usually wider there's more rubber in contact with the ground to further improve grip.

In between the two categories come the vast majority of do-anything MTB tyres. Like most things, tyre choice is down to personal preference. The best all-round tyres will see you through the seasons by gripping in the mud and rolling well through the summer.

Tyre pressures are also important. Decreasing pressure causes the tyre to deform to the shape of the terrain for improved grip and comfort. But if you go too low on pressure you run the risk of pinch-flatting. This is when the inner tube gets caught between the rim and tyre and the rim literally bites through the inner tube causing a flat. This is also called a snakebite puncture because it leaves two small holes in the tube.

Some tyres feature soft strips in the sidewall to reduce the risk of snakebite punctures. Punctures are not uncommon on the mountain bike. Carrying a mini pump and spare tube is important.

When you puncture, remove the tube and run your hand along the inside of the tyre to feel for anything that may have caused it. Do this carefully to avoid slicing your fingers with thorns or shards of glass. Remove whatever has caused the puncture before fitting the new tube.

For emergency tyre split repairs, a strip of tape or even a piece of card placed on the inside of the tyre should get you home. One of the main causes of a puncture is when brake blocks are badly adjusted and end up rubbing a hole in the tyre.

The variety of tyre tread patterns and widths for 26in MTB wheels is never ending, from big knobblies for maximum off-road traction to fast rolling road tyres.

Off-road tyres offer an assortment of tread patterns for different conditions...but you'll still get punctures from time to time. Take care in looking for what's caused the puncture.

Setting up and adjusting gears

Setting up and adjusting gears for trouble-free shifting.

Accurate adjustment of the front and rear gears is essential for fast and precise shifting. It's another one of those procedures that can take minutes if you know what you're doing and will become second nature with practice.

The trick of getting it right is to understand how the shifter relates to and works with the front and rear derailleurs. Shift levers pull and push the gear cable, which in turn operates the derailleurs.

The principle behind correctly adjusting the gears is to adjust the cable tension so that the derailleur shifts the chain into exactly the right position when the shifter is operated. One shift equals one click of the shift lever. This is referred to as 'Indexed' shifting.

Before adjusting the indexing, the stops on the front and rear gears need to be set. The stops (every front and rear derailleur has two tiny 'stop' screws) prevent the derailleurs from shifting too far at the extremes of the gears, when the chain is on the smallest chainring, largest sprocket or the largest chainring, smallest sprocket.

To set the indexing of the rear derailleur, shift to the middle chainring at the front and the smallest sprocket at the rear. Loosen the Allen bolt that holds the gear cable at the derailleur, unscrew the barrel adjuster a few turns, pull the cable tight and re-fasten. Now, shift into the next gear. If the chain doesn't immediately engage the gear make a quarter, anti-clockwise turn of the derailleur's barrel adjuster. If the chain overshifts turn the barrel adjuster a quarter turn clockwise. Keep shifting up and down the gears making quarter turns until the shifting is spot on. Try and picture how the adjustments are affecting the rear gear. Turning the barrel adjuster clockwise moves the rear derailleur away from the wheel, turning it anti-clockwise moves it towards the wheel.

Setting up the front derailleur is very similar, except all adjustments are made at the barrel adjuster on the shifter. Basically, turn the barrel adjuster until the chain stops rubbing the plates of the derailleur.

Some gear mechs only have barrel adjusters on the shifters. Some have them on the mechs and on the shifters. The adjusters on the shifters are useful for making minor adjustments on the move.

If the rear derailleur is proving impossible to index it may be because the derailleur hanger on the frame is bent. They are often replaceable units on aluminium frames. Minor bends on steel frames can be bent back straight, but straightening an aluminium hanger will weaken it.

Adjusting cable tension to fine tune gear shifting is easily done with the barrel adjuster on the rear gear mechanism.

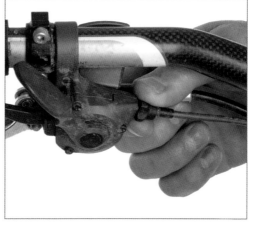

Both front and rear gear mechanisms can also be adjusted for cable tension by using the barrel adjusters on the gear shifters.

Always trim and cap cable ends on gears and brakes.

Setting up and adjusting rim brakes

Getting the best from your brakes.

Rim brakes are reasonably easy to set up and adjust, but worn pads and cable contamination can severely affect their performance. A flagging set of brakes can be brought back to life with correct adjustment and a complete overhaul.

Replacing the cables (and blocks if they're worn) will have the brakes feeling as good as new again. But only use dedicated brake cables and cutters. Regular wire cutters struggle to cut through the thick brake outer. Remove the old cables and cut new outers to the same length as the old, assuming it was the right length. Cutting the brake outer will always produce a little burr. This needs to be filed flat to stop it from interfering with the inner cable.

Squirt a small amount of grease into the cable outer and brake noodle (the aluminium loop that connects the outer cable to the brake caliper). Fit new outer casing caps to the ends and replace the outers on to the frame's cable stops.

Now it's time for the inner cable. Attach the inner cable end nipple at the lever and then thread the cable through the outer casing. Pass it through the brake noodle and fasten it loosely at the brake pinch bolt.

To adjust the brake blocks, first unclip the brake spring. This makes it easier to press the brake caliper against the rim. The pad needs to be centred to the rim's braking surface. Press the caliper against the rim and adjust the pad using a 5mm Allen key. If you have problems with squealing brakes it sometimes helps to toe in the leading edge of the brake pad by 2mm or so.

The inner cable should be adjusted so the brake blocks are clear enough of the rim to avoid rubbing when riding hard (on climbs). Lever feel is a personal thing, but the general consensus is that the brake should start to engage when the levers are pulled about a quarter of the way to the handlebar. When you're happy with the position of engagement secure the inner cable and trim it to length (about 2 inches from the bolt). Tidy up with a cable cap to stop the cable end from fraying.

Operate the brake and check both pads contact the rim at the same time. Balance the brakes by adjusting spring tension. Most brakes have tiny spring tension bolts in the calipers. Screwing them clockwise increases the spring tension and moves the caliper away from the rim.

Lever reach can usually be adjusted via a tiny grub screw located on the lever. Screwing clockwise moves the lever towards the bar.

When you're servicing or adjusting your brakes, inspect the brake cables for any sign of fraying and replace them if they're damaged.

Precise adjustment of brake shoes is absolutely crucial to powerful and safe braking. Take particular care to ensure that the blocks don't touch the tyre or dive towards the spokes when applied.

UK fork manufacturer Pace allow you to fit your brake to the back of the fork. This makes very good mechanical sense. It's odd that no other manufacturers do it.

XTR rim brakes are still the cross country racers choice. When they're well adjusted, the extra power of a disc brake seems superfluous.

Disc brakes

Apart from simple pad replacement, disc brake servicing is usually best left to independent experts. In theory there's nothing to stop an enthusiastic home mechanic from undertaking hydraulic hose bleeds or hose trims, but every brake is different and has its own quirks in both adjustment, bleeds, and repairs.

Hubs, headsets and bottom bracket bearings

Don't forget about the bits on your bike you can't see.

Hubs and cassette freehubs always appear sealed and mysterious. But with a few decent tools it's incredibly easy to service the cone bearings or even replace the freehub. Fortunately, modern units rarely need touching anyway.

Modern bottom bracket units are fully sealed fit and forget items. Some cranks use square tapered axles, some use splined units

Hubs

Most hubs have some form of dust seal protecting the internals. They're usually a rubber or plastic cover and can be carefully prised off using a thin nosed screwdriver. The cones and lockring will now be exposed.

Cone spanners are especially thin so that they can fit on the narrow nut head. You'll need two spanners per hub, one to hold the cone still and the other to loosen the lockring. Shimano front hubs require 13mm/17mm spanners for the cone and lockring, rear hubs need 15mm/17mm.

Remove the lockring and cone from one side followed by the spacers and cone. Lay them out so that you know what order they go back on. Remove the bearings and clean everything with degreaser.

Once the hubs are clean, generously cover the bearing surfaces with top quality (water-resistant) grease and fit the new bearings in both sides. The grease will hold them in place. Carefully insert the axle taking care not to dislodge the bearings.

Loosely screw on the cone, spacer and lockring. You now need to adjust the hub. This is the trickiest part and it can take practice. Screw the loose cone down onto the bearings until it just starts to bind. Back off the cone 1/8th a turn, hold it in place with one cone spanner and tighten the lockring down with the other. You need to get it just right so that the axle turns smoothly without exhibiting any play. Replace the dust cap.

If the hubs run on sealed cartridge type bearings the whole bearing unit will have to be replaced. Some bearings will just lever out, but some require a specific extracting tool, check with the manufacturer.

The 'Aheadset' is a very simple unit. Fit it well, keep it well greased and well adjusted and it'll serve you well for years.

Bottom bracket

These days most bottom brackets (BBs) are disposable cartridge units that need to be replaced when worn out. You need a special BB tool to remove them from the frame and a crank extractor to remove cranks.

CAUTION: Take care when removing the cranks, it's easy to strip the threads if the crank extractor is not properly engaged. When removing the BB, the drive side (the right side when sitting on the bike) unscrews in a clockwise direction and the non-drive unscrews in an anti-clockwise direction.

Headset

To clean the headset, remove the stem and spacers, drop the forks from the bike, remove the old bearings and clean up the cups with degreaser. Bearings are cheap, so it's worth replacing the old ones whenever you service the headset.

Fill the cups with quality grease before replacing the bearings. Make sure all the seals are correctly seated before replacing the forks. You need to preload the bearing in the headset just like the hub bearings. Screw down the top cap over the stem until all bearing play is removed. Lift the front wheel, turn the bars and feel for any binding. If there are any tight spots, slightly loosen the top cap again. When everything is running smoothly and without bearing play, straighten the stem and tighten its bolts.

Basic fork care

Cleaning and maintaining your fork's internals.

A suspension fork is working hard all the time, so it's important to take good care of it. There are lots of different designs on the market, but the majority tend to work along the same principle. A few basic home tweaks should keep them plush. If you're at all worried about servicing them get your local dealer to do the job. Only do it yourself if you can follow the fork manual.

After a season's riding, especially through winter, it pays to change the oil and re-grease or replace the bushings in the lower legs. Before you start, always clean the bike and ideally remove the fork.

Back off any preload pressure, or release the air pressure in air sprung forks. Use a socket to remove the top cap. Remove any springs and pour the old oil into a container. Pump the fork a few times to release any trapped oil. Dispose of the oil at a recycling centre.

Refill with new oil – the manual will give details on how much to use. Fork oil can be bought from most bike dealers. The fork manual should recommend what oil weight to use.

Fork seals and bushings require less frequent attention. It's common to get them serviced at a specialist bike dealer, but you could tackle it at home if you're an enthusiastic mechanic. To get to the bushings you'll have to remove the lower fork legs. You can do this after removing the springs and emptying the fork of oil. Work closely with the manual. To remove the lower legs remove the bolts at the bottom of each leg. This will allow you to slide the fork lowers from the stanchions.

Clean the internals. Hot water and degreaser works best. Inspect seals for any sign of wear. Grease the seals and bushings with a suspension grease. Worn bushings cause the fork to 'knock' on compression.

Working on forks isn't hard if you have a manual to follow, but some experience and mechanical know-how is required. The manuals supplied with the forks are very good at walking you through a service but if in doubt get the dealer to do it. If you've lost the manual most can be downloaded from the manufacturers' websites.

Refer to the manufacturer's instructions, or website, for full information on how to carry out basic servicing on your fork. While we've explained the basics, every fork differs slightly. If in doubt, get a shop to do it.

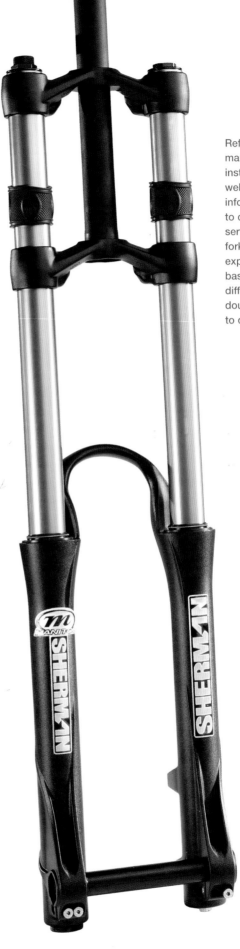

Inspecting for crash damage

Bear the following in mind if you've crashed, or if you're looking to buy a second-hand bike.

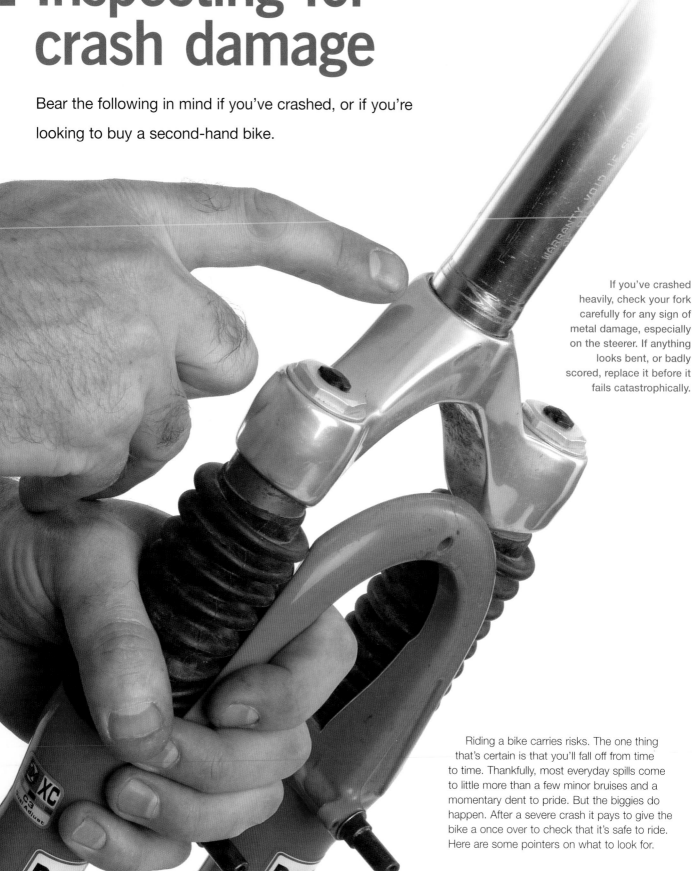

If you've crashed heavily, check your fork carefully for any sign of metal damage, especially on the steerer. If anything looks bent, or badly scored, replace it before it fails catastrophically.

Riding a bike carries risks. The one thing that's certain is that you'll fall off from time to time. Thankfully, most everyday spills come to little more than a few minor bruises and a momentary dent to pride. But the biggies do happen. After a severe crash it pays to give the bike a once over to check that it's safe to ride. Here are some pointers on what to look for.

Check just under the down tube for signs of paint damage or cracks after a crash. Many frames have strengthening gussets here.

Just under the top tube is also an area that's subjected to severe stress in a front-end crash. Again, look for signs of paint damage.

Directly after a crash, get everything running straight before going on your way. The saddle and bars often end up being twisted, brake levers and controls can get knocked out of place. It's a good idea not to overtighten the controls, though, as it allows them to move if they hit the dust.

Frontal impacts are quite common. Some end in a buckled front wheel but in severe cases they can damage the frame and forks. Check to see if the forks are correctly aligned. A big impact will push the fork legs back or damage the junction between the steerer tube and the crown. Inspect the headset to make sure it hasn't been distorted.

Methodically work over the frame looking for any cracks or ripples. Cracks can be quite hard to spot as they are often hairline thin. Look around the welds as this is the most common place for them to occur. If you find anything suspicious stop riding the bike immediately. Some frames are guaranteed for life, but not against crash damage.

It's quite common to bend the rear derailleur hanger in a crash or by knocking the derailleur against an obstacle when riding along. Look at the hanger from behind the bike. It should sit straight and vertical. On most aluminium frames, gear hangers are replaceable. If it's only slightly bent remove the rear derailleur and bend it back using an adjustable spanner. Steel frame hangers are more resilient. They generally don't have replaceable hangers but if a hanger gets damaged it can usually be repaired.

To check a handlebar for damage loosen the stem clamp bolts and slide the bar out of the stem. Inspect the area where the stem grips the bar. If there's any obvious scoring or cracking in the metal you need a new handlebar. Replace it if you have any doubts. If you ride hard, replace your bars and stem every couple of years, even if you haven't crashed.

Make sure your seat post has at least 50mm of extra length pushed inside the main triangle. If you raise it too high, it'll bend the top of the seat tube.

From time to time, and always after a crash, check your handlebar where it's clamped by the stem. Score lines or stress ripples mean it's time to get a new bar.

Index